Acclaim for YOU CAN PRESENT WITH CONFIDENCE

"Paul is way more than a presentation skills coach. His understanding of what drives high-performance individuals will help you build the all-important psychology of a great presenter and turbo-charge your communication to new heights. I have been speaking internationally for nearly ten years. This book has reminded me of the all-important fundamentals, but it's also taught me what I didn't know."

—*Justin Cohen, international speaker and author of* The Astonishing
   Power of Story

"Paul's wealth of practical presentation knowledge is condensed in this book in a manner that is conversational and easy to assimilate. If you speak or present, this book is a 'must have.' You'll read it over and over again."

—*Dan Poynter, CSP, author of more than 120 books*

"This book tells you everything you need to know to be a truly commanding presence on the platform. Paul du Toit has put his stamp of excellence on this book—don't go on stage without reading it."

—*Cathleen Fillmore, author of* The Six Figure Speaker

"Paul dazzles both readers and audiences! Those fortunate to read this book will find practical 'how to' guidance, simple-to-apply steps, and a conversational style. This may well be the definitive guide for presenters to dazzle audiences of their own!"

—*Monica Wofford, CSP, author of* Contagious Leadership
   and CEO, Contagious Companies

"I read your book on the long flight back to Seattle from New York. OUTSTANDING job! It was thorough, complete, highly informative—and fun to read as well!"

—*Bill Stainton, professional speaker and author of*
   The 5 Best Decisions the Beatles Ever Made

YOU CAN
PRESENT

How *to* Speak Like *a* Pro,
Dazzle Your Audience, *and* Get
the Results You Want Every Time

WITH
CONFIDENCE

PAUL DU TOIT

GREENLEAF
BOOK GROUP PRESS

Published by Greenleaf Book Group Press
Austin, Texas
www.greenleafbookgroup.com

First published as Even You Can Present With Confidence
by Congruence Publishing in South Africa in 2008.

Distributed by Greenleaf Book Group LLC

For ordering information or special discounts for bulk purchases, please contact
Greenleaf Book Group LLC at PO Box 91869, Austin, TX 78709, 512.891.6100.

Design and composition by Greenleaf Book Group LLC
Cover design by Greenleaf Book Group LLC

Publisher's Cataloging-In-Publication Data
(Prepared by The Donohue Group, Inc.)

   Du Toit, Paul (Paul Anthony), 1958-
   You can present with confidence : how to speak like a pro, dazzle your audience,
and get the results you want every time / Paul Du Toit. -- 2nd ed.
   p. ; cm.
   ISBN: 978-1-60832-037-0
1. Public speaking. 2. Self-presentation. 3. Persuasion (Psychology) I. Title.
PN4129.15 .D88 2010
808.5/1   2010920420

Part of the Tree Neutral® program, which offsets the number of trees con-
sumed in the production and printing of this book by taking proactive steps,
such as planting trees in direct proportion to the number of trees used:
www.treeneutral.com

TreeNeutral

Printed in China

10 11 12 13 14   10 9 8 7 6 5 4 3 2

Second Edition

For my wonderful daughters,
Chanel and Jenna.

CONTENTS

HOW TO BEST USE THIS BOOK

I recommend using this as a personal reference book you keep at your side. Feel free to make notes in it often, highlighting your important discoveries. Lending your copy to others means parting with your valuable notes, too, so get them to acquire their own copy instead. You'll be doing yourself—and them—a big favor.

Inexperienced presenters (about to embark on your first presentation, have presented infrequently, or have recently received presentation skills training): Read this book from cover to cover using a highlighter to mark the points you want to stress for yourself. Then go back to the sections you highlighted. They will be easy to find as you thumb through the pages. Look for a list of several lessons at the end of each chapter.

Experienced, but never trained in presentation skills: Same as inexperienced presenters.

Experienced presenters (those who have been trained in presentation skills and have gained experience by presenting frequently): Refer to the lessons at the end of each chapter as a guideline to help you select which content you can benefit from the most. Then pick out the chapters that will add the most value to your presentations.

Professional speakers and distinguished Toastmasters: Select the chapters you can learn from most by perusing the Table of Contents.

FOREWORD

What you say is important, yes. But how you say it is extremely important, too.

Like it or not, people give more credence and pay closer attention to an average message that's well presented than an excellent message that's poorly presented.

Ideally, you strive to create an excellent message delivered effectively—providing both substance and style, not one or the other.

In this book, Paul du Toit has demystified what it takes to speak and present well. How? By first helping you understand the challenges you face, providing strategies and tactics for communicating with confidence, then explaining how you can apply them.

As you know, many people—perhaps you too—fear speaking in public. Personally, I *don't* believe the so-called research that says people fear speaking in public more than they fear death. I *do* believe people might fear speaking because their chances of being asked to speak are substantially higher than their chances of dying anytime soon. That makes public speaking a more common fear than death. Knowing how to succeed at speaking goes a long way toward alleviating your fears about it. To that end, this book provides a great service.

Some of what you read in these pages might sound familiar. Good. It's powerful to be reminded of what you know but may not be consistently doing. Its many ideas and insights will feel like a breath of fresh air. "Aha," you'll say, "that's how it is done!"

I suggest reading this book with an eye toward learning what you don't already know. But above all, keep asking, "*How* and *when* will I apply these ideas?" Just as you become an equestrian by riding a horse, you become a speaker by giving speeches. No book, no matter how good, replaces the critical need for practice.

I suggest reading *You Can Present with Confidence* with pen in hand. Write down both key ideas and personal goals on how you'll implement them. Not only is the pen mightier than the sword, the written goal is mightier than the thoughtful aspiration.

Congratulations on picking up this book. You now have strategies and tactics that will give wings to your ideas and sizzle to your future presentations.

—Mark Sanborn, author, *The Fred Factor*
and *You Don't Need a Title to Be a Leader*

INTRODUCTION

It's time to toss the excuses. You too can learn to present like a pro. You can have audiences eating out of your hand, laughing, crying, doing whatever you want.

Whether you're a sales executive, a manager who gives internal presentations, a Toastmaster, a professional speaker, or a lecturer, this book will give you the guidelines you need to deliver presentations that hit the mark every time.

If you are an accomplished professional speaker, you might be curious to see if I have any new tips to offer that will help you to hone your skills further. For the rest of us, let's remind ourselves why we might need them:

People who can verbally project themselves effectively get the best breaks, the best jobs, the quickest promotions—and make the most money.

Look around you. Who represent the success stories? The men and women who command the respect and attention of others. The more respect they command, the more confidence they have—and the higher up the ladder they climb. They may not be the ones who are loyal to the company. They may not have the best brains or be the most organized. But they know how to communicate! And they know how to do it in a way that grabs attention.

Whether it's a job interview, a sales presentation, a speech, or a meeting, the winner is usually the one who can express him or herself best. I'd like that to be you. That is why I have written this book—to give you all the tools and the mental strength you need speak with confidence and to influence people in audiences both great and small.

Effective communicators in high demand

In today's business climate, companies want to employ leaders who can communicate effectively, persuade clients, and influence staff. But there is, and always has been, a shortage of people who can do this. You could fill the gap.

It's no longer just the chief, the CEO, or manager who has to stand before the tribe and gush forth. The world has changed remarkably in the last 100 years. Today, your entire management team, most of the sales force, trainers, negotiators, IT experts, and so on need to know how to communicate effectively. Today, if you don't stand up and speak at least occasionally, you're the exception.

If you want to be an effective member of your team, you'll have to present sometime. But if you've never done it before, I understand your hesitation.

You don't want to make an ass of yourself

We've all been there. We've all emerged from school, college, or university with our heads stuffed with information, ideas, and insights to share with the world. But it all turned into a jumbled mess in our heads when we had to stand up in front of other people and actually articulate our thoughts. The situation could have been a job interview, sharing anecdotes at a friend's wedding, presenting an idea to colleagues, etc.

Oops! Someone has left out a most rudimentary area of your education: how to present yourself. And the interviewer thinks you're an idiot, the wedding guests shuffle uncomfortably, and your colleagues catch a nap . . . or make a mass exodus.

Who in their right mind would want to place themselves in such an embarrassing situation? Don't worry. This can be fixed.

It's not our fault

No one is *born* with presentation skills. A skill, by definition, is something that has to be learned. But during our formal education, no one bothers to teach us some of the most important skills needed in the business world of today, such as the art of speaking properly, using paralanguage and body language, asking questions, or listening properly—the most effective tools available to persuade others to take a specific course of action.

Think about it. In schools, writing is given massive priority. Reading (of which I am a huge fan) is punted with almost as much fervor. Yet an illiterate person who has ambition, drive, and common sense can pay others to do those things for her. And, in reality, most people spend precious little of their working time doing either.

It's the same in the business environment. Despite the emphasis on effective communication today, precious few companies have a policy of developing direct communication skills in their key people—those expected to produce the greatest results. This notwithstanding the fact that presentation-skills training has been globally available for decades.

The result? There are far too many "experienced" presenters around who did not formally learn the rules of presentation. Consequently, a combination of both good and bad presentation habits get passed on through example.

You might be one of those presenters.

Presenting well will save you embarrassment

You will agree that it takes quite a few lessons and considerable practice to learn to drive a car safely. Similarly, it takes time to fashion a good speaker. The very best all started somewhere, usually at the same place they did when they learned to drive. The only difference is that many believe they can pull it off without being trained. That's rather like getting behind the wheel of a car and tackling a 100-mile road trip with no training. If you did something like that with public speaking, you'd have to be either deaf (so as not to hear the loud snoring) or very thick-skinned indeed.

Ironically, the worst culprits are often executives who stand up and bumble on at length, boring their hapless captives with waffling, misplaced humor, appalling irritators, and text-laden slide shows. And few would dare to tell these clueless chaps they've made fools of themselves.

Surprisingly, this even happens to the person who tells such funny jokes around the table at the office year-end party. As soon as he's asked to get up in front of an audience, everything changes. Everything. Why?

Because standing up in front of a captive audience is an unnatural act for anyone who hasn't been groomed to do it. That's why we need to learn the practical "ins and outs" of presentations. No matter how good we are at speaking, we still need training.

Don't get me wrong; the ability to speak well in normal conversation is a huge advantage. However, more presentations bomb due to lack of training (followed by a lack of experience) than for any other reason.

Any successful act you've seen, whether on television or in a show or presentation, has been well prepared and thoroughly rehearsed. The performers have been thoroughly trained, mentored, and coached. It's time to get you pointed firmly in the right direction.

I understand this might be terrifying for you

Delegates often draw me aside at the beginning of a training class or coaching session to confide a truth to me: "You know, Paul, I get very nervous when I have to speak in front of people." It's difficult not to be sympathetic about this fear that seemingly only they experience.

In reality, nearly 100 percent of presenters experience anxiety before going live. The intensity varies from person to person, as does the duration of the anxiety, but it is tempered by experience and confidence. If you've had a bad presenting experience in the past, you may have a particularly intense fear of public speaking.

Let's get past the nerves and on the road to excellence

My task is, of course, to teach you how to redirect your nerves into positive action, using the skills and techniques needed to present with ease and persuasion in a setting made safe to fail at first. My challenge is to convince you that you have it in you to do it well— to help you to see past the fear of social conditioning that results in people:

- Failing to laugh at a joke you tell
- Losing interest while you're explaining something
- Suggesting you were talking "rubbish"
- Not taking you seriously

Positive outcomes result in confidence

Nervousness before a presentation has *nothing* to do with your ability whatsoever. It has *everything* to do with your perceived ability to deliver, your training, your preparation, and your having practiced enough. And when you've built up positive evidence of repeated successes, you can rely on experience too.

This means presentation skills training must be experiential. Delegates who attend my courses deliver live presentations that are videoed. Videos are played back to them and evaluated. They are able to see exactly what they look like on camera, what looks and sounds good, and what doesn't. They make adjustments and try again. They improve.

In this book, I'll outline several ways you can do this on your own or with a group of friends or colleagues.

You'll also learn how to structure a presentation, how to deliver it, what adjustments to make to your voice, how to dress appropriately, how to use relaxation techniques, how to handle questions (even difficult ones), how to add power through decisive gestures, how to use visuals, how to set up equipment, and so on. You should even receive an attitude injection!

As you learn, you'll relax. And your confidence will start growing.

Learning to present brings with it increased assertiveness, a personal belief in yourself, and an awareness of what you do and tend to do when verbally communicating with others. And who knows when you will be asked to step up to the podium? You'll be ready!

CHAPTER 1
BELIEVING YOU CAN

"The greatest danger for most of us is not that our aim is too high and we miss it, but that it is too low . . . and we reach it."

—Renaissance artist Michelangelo

What you put into your head is what will come out

One glorious Highveld summer evening in Johannesburg, I sat with my tennis colleagues on my patio enjoying a welcome beer after playing three challenging sets of tennis. One of them matter-of-factly mentioned that he'd attended presentation skills training a few years previously. The most vivid learning point he remembered—in fact, it hit him right between the eyes—was the need to prepare mentally for a successful presentation.

He put it like this: "We were taught that it's no use standing up to deliver any kind of presentation unless you have the right attitude—the attitude of anticipating success." This, he said, had been a complete revelation to him. He had previously believed in giving the presentation's content all of his attention.

How true! In any presentation—from its preparation to its conclusion—how well you perform has everything to do with bringing positive mental energy to the task. First and foremost, presenting is about confidence. So the most important tool you need to pull it off well is trust in your own ability—trust grounded in self-belief.

> "You will never change your life until you change your belief about what you are capable of."
> —Leadership speaker Robin Crow
> from his book *Jump and the Net Will Appear*

Decide you can do it

Deciding upfront to put together and deliver a compelling presentation with a positive attitude will set you firmly on the road to success. The reason is quite simple, really. People who set clear goals tend to achieve them because their brains take instructions from their subconscious minds to accomplish what they set their minds to do.

If you approach any task with the conviction that you can succeed, your brain will demand a strategy that enables you to achieve what you've set out to do. Without a clear conviction, you can expect inconsistent progress and dubious results. So your best starting point is making a clear decision.

The manner in which you approach a presentation has much to do with these factors:

- The beliefs you hold about yourself and your presenting ability
- What you have done to address those beliefs
- How close you are to believing you have what it takes to pull off a convincing presentation

Let me explain these in detail.

We adopt our beliefs about ourselves at an early age and in a random fashion. Specifically, we formulate opinions about ourselves at key moments. A teacher telling six-year-old Johnny "put down your hand, Johnny; Sarah will recite the poem for us" can have a chilling effect on Johnny's self-confidence. If this statement is followed by encouragement, a different outcome is likely, but if it's followed by further discouragement, Johnny will believe he's not good enough to stand up and recite the poem. He'll believe that Sarah will always be preferred because she must be better. In the future, he won't speak up at all to avoid the pain of rejection.

For many people, this kind of scenario sparked their anxiety around speaking. It need not be so.

Your first attempt at speaking in front of your classmates can be quite harrowing. What pops out can be as unexpected as it is random. Today, it's dangerous to assume you will be less nervous as an adult than you were as a child. Emotions are time travellers.

Psychologically, we draw on past experiences to anticipate reactions we're likely to get. Past bad experiences teach us to expect rejection. In turn, this expectation robs us of our ability to present with confidence. So the adult who suffered failure in the past is likely to meet with limited success when attempting to speak with authority in front of an audience—at least until that early programming changes.

Positive experiences will ground your self-belief

One gains confidence by having positive experiences, which provide hard evidence that you can, in fact, do what you'd believed you couldn't do. When your belief system changes, your outcomes change.

But you can't gain positive experiences without putting yourself "out there." This means you have to pluck up your courage and decide to grab the presenting opportunities that come your way. Once you have a good grasp of the techniques in this book, I suggest forming small groups and practicing on one or two friends—people you know are on your side. Ask for feedback about what worked and what didn't work. If their comments are critical, remember they're criticizing your *technique*, not you as a person. Then try again. The more you keep at it, the more you'll improve and the easier it will seem.

When you feel ready, accept presenting opportunities that come your way at work. Don't hesitate. Just do it!

You'll find that when friends or colleagues respond positively to your presentations, your confidence grows. You can then challenge yourself to get better and try new things. Watch other presenters with a critical eye, identifying techniques you liked and didn't like. What did you think was convincing? Would you trust what these presenters had to say enough to buy products from them?

As your skills build and your confidence increases, so will your self-belief. When you deliver a presentation with no doubt about your ability to do so in a compelling way, audience members will feel it. For some presenters, this happens quickly; for others, it takes longer. But through patience, practice, and perseverance, you will get it right.

It's important to understand that initial botched attempts are completely normal and nothing to be ashamed of. It doesn't mean you are a failure; it just means you still have to hone your skills. Many of today's best speakers progressed slowly at first, but achieved increasing degrees of competence through perseverance and experience. The tragedy is that many give up without giving themselves a sporting chance.

You are allowed to be "you"

Here is the first and most vital truth you need to accept: *You are allowed to be yourself when presenting.* The speakers who affect me the strongest are those who are simply themselves. They speak from the heart, sharing what they have to say with others. Those who are obviously performing don't come across as authentic and leave me feeling confused.

Of course, it's easy to be yourself when you're chatting to friends. Presenting requires an infinitely more complex set of actions, often with more significant consequences. The irony is that most people instinctively perform the actions necessary to present when involved in informal dialogue with others, but lose it when in front of a "formal" audience.

Take the office joker, for example. Imagine that you're at a social gathering. Harry's in a good mood and people are talking about football, which he knows plenty about. Harry launches into an animated description of a match in which a goalkeeper missed a back pass, resulting in an embarrassing faux pas. Everyone around him roars with laughter. You see, Harry was telling a story about something that actually happened on a subject with which he was familiar. True to life, perhaps embellished, but well received! He was rewarded by the laughs he received. But put an untrained Harry in front of an audience presenting a brief on his company's product to potential buyers, and it's like an alien arrived. He acts quite differently than the confident, joking Harry having a beer with his friends.

Why? It's simple really: speaking conversationally with friends is natural and feels familiar; a presentation feels unnatural because it's staged. So instead of being ourselves, we try to be what we think we need to be. The truth is that being ourselves will do just fine, thanks!

Most people play themselves very well indeed, but only actors, and good ones at that, succeed in playing other people convincingly. So either we need to learn to act, or we need to learn to be ourselves in unnatural situations.

Enthusiasm is key

One of the best ways to prove you can speak to an audience with confidence is to prepare a short talk about your favorite hobby. You see, when people are given an opportunity to speak about something they feel passionate about, they speak with enthusiasm and their true ability becomes evident. The overall result is authenticity. If you can produce a credible speech when fuelled by passion for your favorite topic, you have the potential to convey this authenticity in any speech or presentation.

One time, I watched a mature man in a management position present in an unconvincing and shy manner. So apologetic was his delivery, I doubt that a child would have accepted a free ice cream sundae from him. At the break, I struck up a conversation with him. He told me how he had recently been passed over for promotion. If everyone in the room could have experienced the passion in his words brought on by the hurt he was feeling as I did, we would have observed someone who indeed possessed the ability to speak with authenticity.

If you've ever witnessed a technically competent presentation and wondered why you weren't convinced by it, it's likely the presenter lacked enthusiasm. But beware of the converse—too much enthusiasm or overkill. Audiences quickly read insincerity in any attempt at forced enthusiasm.

You've probably purchased something you didn't really need because you were persuaded it was a good idea at the time. What persuaded you? Logic? Unlikely. More than likely, the salesperson's *enthusiasm* hooked you.

Enthusiasm is a vital presentation tool, particularly when it's authentic and not overdone, and also when the presenter truly believes in its benefits and result. There's tangible excitement! So how can you apply this principle? Know your subject well, have a clear idea about how you'll put your exciting message across, and then deliver it with passion. You'll be irresistible!

Moving into the zone

A while back, I was delivering a public seminar in East London on the east coast of South Africa. Although the function coordinator had been given a full list of my requirements, I arrived at the venue to find the setup far from complete. To start with, the door was locked. I wasted what seemed like an eternity arranging for it to be opened. Then my "locksmith" disappeared! So instead of being free to set up my equipment, I was reduced to moving tables and chairs to create a reception area. Shortly before my guests were due to arrive for registration, the hotel staff sauntered in with no sense of urgency whatsoever.

Mustering all my assertive powers, I created enough urgency to get events moving in the right direction, then found a manager to take control of the "front of house" situation. This freed me to set up my presentation equipment. By the time I was happy with the room setup and all my equipment was working, I had only fifteen minutes before the beginning of my talk. I was not in the best frame of mind; I needed to get "into the zone." So I walked upstairs on the esplanade into the fresh air and spent the next eight minutes taking in the sea, the rocks, the waves, and the gulls while doing this bit of earnest self-talk:

I have to remember that my audience is in no way responsible for the shambles at reception. These people have not only paid good money, but they've set aside precious time to come and hear me speak. What an honor! What a privilege! Today, I will deliver the most powerful, energetic, convincing, and humorous talk I've ever delivered.

And I did. To this day, that talk stands out as one of my most highly rated by a public audience. It proved that I could take control of my emotions—and you can too!

Dealing with success

It's wonderful to pull off a presentation that produces the result I want. I'm a strong advocate of celebrating successes because it reinforces one's self-belief and helps "groove" winning behaviors, just as tennis players "groove" their stroke mechanics.

But it's important never to lose your humility. No one has "arrived" after just one victory. The true test of champions is being able to repeat their performances over and over again. The techniques in this book can help you develop the skills to win consistently, over and over again!

It's essential to maintain perspective and humility. Giving a great presentation one day doesn't automatically mean your next one will be fabulous. With a different audience, a different place, and different needs, you'll have to perform well all over again. The saying "you are only as good as your last presentation" isn't a cliché for nothing.

Dealing with failure or rejection

By the same token, it's helpful to understand rejection and develop an ability to put it into perspective. We do not fail because we are useless; we fail because we still have lessons to learn. The argument "I'm no good at public speaking" is usually based on ignorance, false information, and poor attitudes. Anyone who can hold a conversation can learn to speak well in public; it just takes some learners longer than others.

As a student of effective public speaking skills, you'll also find out quickly that only those who apply themselves get good at it! So take any setbacks in stride. (Of course, this takes courage too.)

Reverse the way you view rejection

I once watched a life insurance salesman take the stage at his company's annual sales convention to accept the prize as man of the year, beating more than 900 other salesmen to earn the award. As he clutched his trophy, he announced to the spellbound audience that he was, in fact, a failure. "In reality," he went on, "I'm the biggest failure of all of you here tonight. You see, I knocked on many more doors than you likely did this year. And I don't think you could possibly have had as many doors slammed in your face or as many 'no's' as I did. But that's why I'm holding this trophy tonight and you're not—because I was prepared to take the rejection. I learned long ago that every 'no' I get takes me one step closer to my next 'yes'."

His colleagues gave him a standing ovation.

"We do not believe in ourselves until someone reveals that something deep inside us is valuable, worth listening to, worthy of our trust, sacred to our touch. Once we believe in ourselves we can risk curiosity, wonder, spontaneous delight or any experience that reveals the human spirit."

—e.e.cummings, novelist and poet

Professional speaker and author **Simon T. Bailey** gives this insight into the value of having a rock-solid self-belief:

I've discovered that, whatever the context, every rejection is one step closer to an acceptance. It only takes one person or organization to believe, one person or organization to catch the vision. You need merely hold onto the thread of belief, even when there is nothing else to hold on to.

What you believe decides the course of your life. As you believe, so you become. You don't decide your future. You decide what you believe; what you believe drives your behavior; and your behavior creates your future.

Understand that not everyone will "get you" or "buy" your presentation. There will be many people—too many people—who won't agree with you or understand your message or want your product. Too often we see this as rejection and fail to put it into proper context.

I'm inviting you to step out in faith. Move forward with your proposal. Request the raise or the promotion you deserve. Ask that certain someone to lunch. Try to sell your invention. Pitch your new idea. Some will buy you, others won't. But being rejected simply adds another layer to your experience. It's how you view it and what you do with it that makes the difference.

—Simon T. Bailey, author of *Release Your Brilliance*
www.simontbailey.com

KEY LESSONS FROM CHAPTER 1

If you enthusiastically believe you can prepare and deliver a great presentation that achieves your intended results, then that's what is likely to happen. You are using the power of autosuggestion to put yourself on track.

1. Eliminate negative programming relating to your presentation's potential. It's almost always false and based on someone else's opinion—and usually ignorance.

2. Take advantage of any and all opportunities to develop your public speaking or presentation skills. Having positive presenting experiences will increase your confidence.

3. Your audience will be able to detect whether you feel confident or nervous, so you owe it to both audience members and yourself to develop your confidence.

4. You are allowed to be yourself. You don't have to "perform" to be effective.

5. Genuine, authentic enthusiasm is infectious and can be cultivated. You'll know when you meet someone who has charisma; the underlying quality is enthusiasm.

6. Get yourself "into the zone" mentally before a presentation. Focus on being excited about your delivery, your product, and your objective, and get rid of worries or fears. Once the day has arrived, it's too late for negative feedback—simply put your best foot forward.

7. If a presentation bombs, it doesn't mean you are useless; it merely means that you still have a few lessons to learn. People learn more from a presentation that went wrong than from one that went right.

CHAPTER 2
OVERCOMING THE 5 GREAT FEARS

"Worry is like a rocking chair—it will give you something to do, but it won't get you anywhere."

—Anonymous

Why feel nervous about presenting?

Before going any further, let's look at those nerves presenters keep telling me about.

First, let me say that I know how you feel. I used to get nervous too. I'd get a choking feeling in my throat, my voice and hands would tremble, and I'd feel nauseous before having to speak in front of an audience. These symptoms dissipated over time. So what changed?

Well, for a start, I just got up and started speaking, despite the nervousness. And the more I did it the better I got. This is because, first, I learned to channel my nervous energy into positive action. Secondly, the more I honed my skills, the more confident I became. Thirdly, in the process of getting on with it, I discovered the reasons for my nerves were actually erroneous. These reasons were what I call "The Five Great Fears." Let's look at these fears one by one.

The five great fears

I have identified what I refer to as "The Five Great Fears" that people experience in front of an audience, whether it be to act, present, or do any form of public speaking. They are:

1. What will people think of me if I fail?
2. What if I lose my way during my presentation?
3. What if I don't have enough compelling, convincing content?
4. What if I come undone during question time?
5. What if they get bored while I'm speaking?

How can these fears be overcome?

1. What will people think of me if I fail?

"A man cannot be comfortable without his own approval."
—American writer Mark Twain

Why do we become afraid, jittery, and nervous? It is simply this: *We are all concerned, to a greater or lesser degree, about what people will think of us.*

This fear has become so embedded in the human psyche that it has been etched into our culture in the expression "losing face"—a saying that originated with the Chinese. When you present, you assume a moral high ground, that of a subject authority. The fear of "losing face" is related to losing *mianzi* (Chinese) meaning authority, thus rendering your credibility questionable in the minds of those in your audience. Without credibility, your presentation is worthless. Instinctively we know this, and it causes many presenters significant stress.

From prehistoric days, cavemen and women have sat around a fire or rock chatting and socializing, much like we'd do today around a table. But having to stand up and talk to others formally sets up a completely different ball game that's historically reserved for the leader of the tribe (who only found it easy to do through experience, among other things). The risk of "messing up" and "losing face" has always loomed large.

Now let's be realistic. When you attend a presentation, either by choice or requirement, do you want the speaker to make a total idiot of himself or herself so you can sit back and snigger? That's your first reality check. After all, few people take pleasure in another's failure. Most people are like you and me—we want the best for one another. Why should it be any different when you get up to speak?

First, remember this: **People in your audience would rather you give positive feedback than negative.** They're on *your* side. They don't wait for you to mess up so they can guffaw with mirth (well, not usually).

Second, everyone begins life without any skills. It might be hard to believe, but neither Roger Federer nor Steffi Graf could play tennis the day they were born. Nor could Tiger Woods play golf. They all had to learn their craft from scratch. I understand that you already know this, but perhaps you haven't applied this to learning how to present properly. So, when starting out, simply **accept that you are a beginner** and that's okay.

Yes, some people may show a natural ability for public speaking, but it's rare to meet someone who doesn't need coaching. You'll find that those who've had access to public speaking or drama classes at school have a head start over others, so if you have children, it's a good idea to encourage them to get involved in public speaking at school. In fact, I think age four is a good time to start, but there's nothing wrong with age forty-four either.

Third, **you're allowed to improve at your own pace**. When mothers of toddlers get together, it's interesting to see the embarrassed reaction of the mom whose fourteen month old is still crawling while all the other kids are already walking, or the thirty month old who's still wearing diapers. I've advised anxious moms that they needn't worry; by the time their kids are eighteen years old, they will be walking, perhaps even running, and will no longer require diapers. When we realize that people reach milestones in their own good time, it takes the pressure off.

Fourth, **accept that not everyone will like everything you say or do**, and that's okay. Assuming you're the world's most engaging speaker, approximately 3 percent of the people who see you still won't like some aspect of what you say or do. Extensive research of speakers, trainers, and presenters indicates that consistent ratings of over 96 percent are rare and 97 percent unheard of. *You are thereby released from the burden of having to be perfect.* What a relief!

Releasing yourself from others' opinions is another major step toward speaking and presenting confidently. Some say it's none of your business what other people think of you, that their opinion of you reflects who *they* are more than who *you* are.

You can further relieve pressure by gaining a fresh perspective. If your presentation bombs and you don't get the business or approval you want, **there'll be another day**, another audience, and another presentation. People quickly get over you and move on, so do the same—but not without learning from the experience and applying what you've learned to your next presentation.

Failure helps everyone improve while it weeds out winners from losers. Your reaction to failure is far more important than the failure itself. In sports, you'll find that those who break the biggest records had to break the failure records first make it to the top.

Also remind yourself that **this is not a competition**. There will always be someone with a better voice, a cleverer structure, or even a superior product to yours. A football team that wins the league seldom does so without losing a few matches along the way. Although the losses hurt, they keep the players sharp.

Focusing on audience needs also helps with nerves. Remember, your **presentation is not about you** or your being liked. It's about sharing an important idea with audience members. So take your focus off yourself and channel your energy into getting your point across effectively. Give your listeners a powerful experience.

This, of course, requires the process of learning—practically and methodically—how to present, finding out where your weak points are, and going about putting them right. And this process is a one-step-at-a-time journey to help you get good at talking **to** people, rather than **at** them.

The process of learning to present well includes these six steps:

- Understanding all the rules of presenting
- Preparing adequately (not only your content, but your visuals and yourself as well!)

- Practicing before going live
- Delivering the presentation
- Receiving feedback
- Acting on the feedback

2. What if I lose my way during my presentation?

The second greatest fear is this: "What if I go blank, rearrange the order, or leave out an important chunk of my presentation?!"

The best way to overcome this fear is to **use cue cards**. Most presenters buy and use a pack of index cards for this purpose. Having cue cards on hand is by no means taboo in the world of presenting. Some believe one should never present with cue cards at all. If you get paid to speak, then I agree. If not, using cue cards correctly can be a welcome friend, so go right ahead and use them! I see no harm in professional speakers using cue cards rehearsing a new talk, and then having them on hand for that maiden delivery "just in case."

Referring to cue cards can keep you on track, particularly for untried presentations, and thus take pressure off you. Also, audience members subconsciously regard cue cards as a positive sign that the presenter is organized, has a structure, and is less likely to exceed the time. So don't worry about looking unprepared. Use cue cards if needed, but don't regard them as compulsory.

If you're using PowerPoint slides, cue cards can help you introduce the next point *before* you bring up the relevant slide. Doing this leaves a strong impression. Conversely, when you introduce the slide that's already up on the screen, it shows you're likely reading it. In the meantime, you're minimizing vital eye contact and risking losing audience attention.

This brings us to one of our "don'ts." The most common response to this particular fear is creating a detailed PowerPoint show and then reading points off the screen or monitor. But reading your presentation word for word is acutely boring for the listeners.

Instead, format your cue cards carefully and correctly. The more writing you have to refer to, the more you will come across as reading, the less eye contact you will make, and the faster you will lose your audience. So prepare no more than six trigger-point sentences per cue card. Write them in bold and preferably in lower case. Number each card in case you accidentally drop them and have to put them back in order quickly. Hold them by the corner of the cards or in the palm of your hand.

If you're at a presentation skills course and your facilitator insists that you use cue cards, then do so, even if you would prefer not to. The intention is to help you develop this skill for when you really need it. Don't feel you have to always use them, but one day, you might be glad you've practiced with them. If you decide to use them, make sure you do two or three practice runs in advance. It's easy to forget what a trigger word was supposed to trigger, so practicing with the cards sorts that out.

3. What if I don't have enough compelling, convincing content?

In reaction to this fear, many people overcompensate by preparing far too much. The logic is to prepare about 15 percent more content than will be required—just in case. But the reality is that it's the exception rather than the rule that your presentation will start on time or that you'll get all of your promised time allocation. If you have more information to get across than time to deliver it in, you'll likely get to the middle of your talk having given barely a third of its content. You're then likely to panic and speed up the pace, risking rattling off the rest of your presentation rapidly and losing your audience. What a sweat! And what a waste!

Assuming you're an authority on the topic you're presenting, you could probably speak five hours without batting an eyelid. But most listeners will only be able to remember a few main points. So select from your vast resource of knowledge only the information required by the audience to make a decision. *Only that information*, no more.

Prepare your presentation to end five minutes before your allocated amount of time. Practice two to three times in front of a mirror to make sure you deliver your content at an easy, even pace—with conviction. When you review your content, cut out the points that aren't critical to swaying a decision. **You need to tell audience members only what they need to know in order to decide.** As Coco Chanel so famously said about perfume, "Less is more." The same applies to your presentation.

4. What if I come undone during question time?

You may be afraid of getting caught without all the answers when it's time to entertain audience questions. The fear? You'll look stupid.

To understand why so many seemingly good presentations come undone during question time, the poser "why have question time at all?" needs to be answered. Well, **you don't have to have question time**. Often it's included out of habit or because it's the way it's always done.

Also, when questions are called for, the presenter usually thinks the objective is to allow the audience to voice concerns or request clarification. Although this might happen or might be what audience members want, it's not the presenter's key objective.

Including an allocated question time should be to handle uncertainties, remove doubts about the validity of your standpoint, and/or close the business. If this isn't the outcome, it's likely the presenter has no training or experience in how to handle questions.

Always approach a Q&A session prepared with a technique for handling questions and ready answers for anticipated issues not addressed during the presentation. (I will discuss a specific technique for this in Chapter 10.) Let me make this comment to alleviate your fear: **you don't have to know all the answers**. It's all right to say, "I'm not sure about that. Could I do some research and get back to you on that one?"

5. What if they get bored while I'm speaking?

Perhaps the most humiliating experience a presenter could endure is to lose one's audience. It's easy to tell when audience members have disengaged from you. They converse among themselves, write without looking up, or text-message on their cell phones. Then there's the inevitable shuffling and fidgeting. Your fear of being embarrassed in this way is quite legitimate.

Here's what you can do to ensure these activities don't happen.

- Make eye contact from the start.
- Be enthusiastic.
- Believe in your topic and let your enthusiasm shine through.
- Believe in yourself.
- Deliver your message with clarity.
- Add pauses to your content.
- Use humor appropriately.
- Talk with purpose on every point without waffling.
- Give your presentation a logical structure.

To carry this off, proper preparation is required, especially speaking clearly without waffling and having a logical structure. When the big moment arrives and you're standing before your audience ready to begin, that's the moment you establish eye contact.

Don't just launch into your speech. Pause for a moment. Create a "space" for your presentation. Take in the people in the audience and let them take you in. Accept their receptive expectation. This will help you to feel their support. It will also communicate that you see them. That way, they know you're not just spouting words; you're speaking to *them*.

Doing this will also tell them you feel comfortable being yourself. It will give them confidence in you, which will in turn boost your confidence in yourself. If you establish and maintain this personal contact throughout, you will keep their attention.

Once you've created the right atmosphere, begin speaking confidently, allowing your enthusiasm to shine through when appropriate. Pause at appropriate moments to let key ideas sink in. Don't forget to look people in the eye.

If using humor isn't your forte, leave it out. Many a powerful presentation has been expertly delivered without any humor at all. But don't be thrown if people laugh at unexpected moments. This usually means they identify with something you've said, even if you didn't intend it to be funny. If this happens, pause. Continue when the laughter has died down completely.

Conversely, if you're good at being humorous, use that talent. Flaunt what you've got, but within reason. Remember, your primary objective to get your point across. Getting a laugh is a pleasant bonus, but must be secondary to your primary objective.

Remember that your unique personality, above all else, will ensure the success of your presentation. You're quite good enough without pretending to be someone else!

The best way to relax

Ever considered where vocal sounds come from? They come from the muscles in and around the diaphragm pushing air out of the lungs, through the trachea, over the vocal chords, and out through the mouth. We've become so skilled at using our voices that we can fashion sounds to come out exactly as we please. It's funny, then, that when we present, these sounds don't quite come out as we intended.

So a few minutes before going live, take in five deep breaths through the nose, hold for two seconds, then let the air out slowly through the mouth. After doing this, your brain will be better powered, your diaphragm exercised, and your nerves settled.

I asked **Alvin Law**, a certified speaking professional and Hall of Fame member of the Canadian Association of Professional Speakers (CAPS), to share some of his experiences with me. As you will discover, there's something different about Alvin.

Because I was born without arms, I didn't have a great many career options. Indeed, I had learned great skills using my feet and, by the end of high school, was completely independent. The challenge was a 1970s society in need of enlightenment. Since that wasn't going to happen quickly, I decided to adapt myself to society and, with the profound assistance of a school counselor, I enrolled in a broadcasting and communications course at a large college in Canada.

Two years later, I graduated with honors (a shock to my parents). Armed (pardon the pun) with a diploma from a reputable school, I scooped up an on-air job as a disc jockey at a popular new FM rock-radio station in Regina, Saskatchewan. It really was a plum job and, again surprising everybody, I was quickly promoted. My popularity soared. I was even invited to a junior high school career fair and asked to speak to a classroom of young adolescents. Speak to people?! Worse yet . . . speak to teenagers?!

You see, I got into radio to hide my deformed body from a rude world, plus my cool "rock" voice made me feel, well . . . cool! (By the way, at twenty years old, I was decidedly "uncool.") Nevertheless, I had to go and speak—station manager's orders.

So I was trusted with the Rock 92 van, wore my Rock 92 vinyl jacket, and passed out Rock 92 stickers. I was introduced by a thirteen year old and, just like that, I was about to give my first speech. This wasn't in my master plan!

I didn't bother writing anything down. I thought I'd just wing it. By ten minutes in, the students all looked at me with this zombie-like stare. Not knowing anything about speaking to groups, I thought, "Right . . . they like to ask questions in these sessions." So I blurted out, "Do you guys have any questions?" Instantaneously, almost all the hands went up. Yikes!! I acknowledged one boy and, without any hesitation, he asked, "How do you go to the bathroom?" I didn't see that one coming! Man, how do I answer a question like that?

Well, I did answer and, yes, I can go to the bathroom but it takes patience and creativity. Pants with elastic waistbands help. But the point is, if you're not ready to answer any possible question, you need to work on your content. I would advise that speaking to kids can be the best learning ground. I may be simplifying things but if you can deliver your talk to varying ages of students in their classrooms and make them understand your material, you're well on your way to explaining it to everyone. Remember, simple is a good thing!

By the way, that one classroom speech started me on a path that has seen me speak to more than two million people. If you're wondering, I haven't done Q&A for more than ten years but not because I won't. After thousands of questions, I have built the answers into my content. It's simple again; you're there for the audience, not the other way around.

—Alvin Law, author of *Alvin's Laws of Life*
www.alvinlaw.com

KEY LESSONS FROM CHAPTER 2

1. Audience members want you to succeed, just as you want other presenters to do well.

2. It's okay to be a beginner and improve at your own pace.

3. Don't concern yourself with what others think of you. You will know if you have prepared adequately.

4. It's alright to make mistakes—but learn from them.

5. It's normal to feel nervous before a presentation. What counts is how you channel your nervous energy. Do this by focusing on giving your audience a good experience.

6. Using cue cards helps you overcome your fear of getting lost during the presentation. Don't read and rely on your PowerPoint slides to stay on track.

7. Don't worry about having too little content. You usually need less than you think. Apply the principle "less is more."

8. Use deep breathing exercises before starting your presentation to relax yourself.

9. Don't fear being caught off guard by difficult questions. If you're the subject expert and you're prepared, you'll be able to answer most questions. For the ones you can't, simply be honest and say, "I don't know but I'll find out."

There is no substitute for experience, but make sure it's against a background of learning the correct principles. The more experience you have, the easier it becomes to channel your nerves into positive energy that serves you.

CHAPTER 3
SETTING A CLEAR OBJECTIVE

"Whenever you deliver a presentation, ask yourself: What is my purpose? What do I want to achieve? Am I here to entertain, persuade, motivate, or inform?"

—Marlene Ward, Distinguished Toastmaster
and presentation skills coach

You'll get exactly what you aim for

For many presenters, getting ready for a presentation simply means preparing a slide show, setting out to make it—and themselves—look professional. And when the intended objective (e.g., a call to action, a sale, a changed viewpoint) is not reached, they're surprised and disappointed. But why be surprised? When you prepare with the sole aim of looking professional, that's all you're likely to get. You can only achieve the specific outcome you want if you properly plan for it.

Take note: A slide show on its own is *not* a presentation. Consider it a visual tool that, if used with skill, can enhance your message and help you to attain the outcome you seek. And that is all it is. The trick many (dare I say *most?*) presenters miss is that preparing for a presentation involves many steps; putting together a slideshow is only one of those steps. Setting a clear objective is the most vital starting point.

When the aim is just to get through it . . .

For many people faced with having to give a presentation, it's completely normal to try to get out of doing it. So, please believe me, when you're cornered like a rat in a trap, it's natural to respond by creating a 457-slide PowerPoint show, feverishly working on it into the early hours the day you're due to present it. Surely your dazzling show with animated airplanes that fly and explode on landing will keep 'em awake! Of course you've left no time to practice, but no worries—you can read right off the screen, your back to the audience, as you look to just getting through it.

So you drag yourself to the presentation on two hours sleep (if you're lucky) and then stress yourself into a cardiac seizure because the equipment you need isn't in place and the technician nowhere in sight. You complete the set-up with impatient audience members looking on. Finally you get going 20 minutes late. Considering the shaky start, you do well to settle down quickly. Within five minutes, you're in your stride reading off 457 slides, still with your back to the audience. "After all, everyone knows I'm the expert," you think. Then you wonder why people are dozing in the darkened room (that is, those who are still there).

Nothing wrong with *you;* it's just 437 slides too many.

Realize that "getting through" a presentation is ego-based and only answers questions like "How did I do?" and "Did people like me?" Though it's gratifying to get a few laughs and deliver a technical masterpiece, this falls way short of why you'd slave for hours preparing only the PowerPoint presentation.

What's the purpose of your presentation?

When getting caught up in the mechanics of putting together, rehearsing, and delivering a presentation, it's easy to forget this critical question: "What is my key objective?"

But when you've finished speaking, lights switched off and room empty, what exactly should your listeners do as a direct result of your talk? Whatever visuals you create, however you dress, and whatever logistical arrangements you make—it's critical to direct every action toward realizing your key objective. Or why bother at all?

Question anything that detracts from or fails to support your key objective and possibly leave out those parts. Sometimes it's hard to cut out a favorite joke or clever anecdote, but too bad. You must do it—that is, if you're serious about successfully delivering on your key objective.

What is the desired result of a presentation?
Simply for listeners to take action on what you've said.

There are various kinds of presentations and a myriad of categories, too. A talk can range from presenting a paper to doing a recital, making a political speech to delivering a keynote. It can involve conducting training, kicking off a product, doing a business presentation, or addressing the PTA—to name just a few. All presentations have a purpose, a definite objective.

So before you sit down to plan yours, determine your objective by answering this first question: *"What do I want audience members to do immediately after the presentation?"*

Once you've established the outcome you want, plan how to set up your close to ensure audience members do what you suggest. Then plan what resources you'll need, how you'll put it all together, and how you'll structure your content within the time frame available. You'll find that beginning with your objective in mind makes your preparation easier and your talk flow more logically.

The second question to ask is this: *"What will I do to remind them afterward?"*

This is especially important when you need more than one step to put your suggestions into action. It is also important as a backup in case people don't do as you suggested, or if a required group consensus wasn't reached. To remind them, you could suggest deadlines or timelines in your close, then follow up with calls, letters, postcards, or emails to key audience members. Get these reminders to arrive at just the right time so people will take the required action. Maybe you'll need to schedule a follow-up presentation that features a longer Q&A session.

Consider your options in the planning stages, so you have clarity on (1) what you're aiming for and (2) what you need to do to meet your key objective.

Paul Bridle, Certified Speaking Professional and Past President of the Global Speakers Federation (2003–2004), shares his philosophy on presentation objectives:

Two types of objectives for any kind of presentation can be identified by asking the following questions:

1. What do you want the listeners to do as a result of what you give them? The operative words are *to do*. In most cases, you aren't giving people knowledge for the sake of knowledge. You are giving them knowledge because of what you want them *to do* with that knowledge. So your key objective answers this question: "What will the listeners be motivated to do as a result of what I say?" I am overt about this and tell people what I want them to do. At the very least, I say they're expected to take one thing away from the presentation that they'll use. It has a powerful influence on listeners when you ask them to take action.

2. How do you want to feel as a result of this presentation? I am a big believer in giving added value, so I ask, "What sort of presentation would I give if I were being paid three times what I'm being paid for this presentation?" Mentally answering this question can raise your game considerably. In my case, it gives me a rush of adrenaline and gets me out there primed to deliver at a higher level.

—Paul Bridle, leadership methodologist, author of *Question Your Thinking*, www.paulbridle.com

This is true no matter the audience size

Can an audience be one person? Yes, it most certainly can. You would simply use different techniques to present one-on-one or one-on-two or one-on-many. Thinking that effective presentation skills apply only to one-on-many presentations shows a misunderstanding of what a presentation really is.

> **What is a presentation?**
> An opportunity to convince an audience of an idea, concept, or product.

Your presentation method may vary from a one-on-one discussion at a table to a full-blown presentation in a boardroom or auditorium. Its nature is driven by the environment, circumstances, and objectives of the parties involved.

Two people in a dialogue might have different objectives, but could end up agreeing on the same solution. One person might require a service solution while the other needs a product. If the product meets the other person's need, differing motivations can still result in a deal being clinched.

What are common objectives?

Kinds of objectives for a presentation could involve a call to action, a sale, or a request to consider an alternate viewpoint. Let's look at three examples.

For CEOs, a presentation to employees might include a request or call to action to start implementing a new strategic plan.

For a young man, the most important presentation he'll ever make is to his girlfriend's father asking him for her hand in marriage. How important it is to get that presentation right and "make the sale!" (But also important is ensuring that his conduct leading up to the presentation aligns with the outcome he wants.)

Whatever your audience will be, your answer to the question "What am I trying to achieve?" provides the direction you need to prepare your content.

Address their problem with your value proposition

Whether or not you use presentations to sell, market, or show-case a product or service, consider this simple question: *If you're presenting to a group of people, surely it's because you ultimately want them to do something, right?* Even if you're not selling a product or service, at least you want to persuade them to the merits of your point of view.

Still, if you're trying to convince people of something they're not interested in, they won't listen to you. So, when will people listen to you? They listen when you address *their problem*. And when and why do people buy? They buy when they are convinced that *your solution or value proposition* will solve their problem.

So, if you already have the product, service, or idea, ask, "*Whose* problem will this most likely address and *how* it will solve the problem?" Then design your presentation to offer a solution (or value proposition) to those in the target market you've identified.

Remember, saying *how* your solution will solve their problem is far more enticing than describing *what* a product or service can do. Be sure to build your content based on this time-tested concept called "sell benefits, not features." To help you do that, you can design your presentation using the following five steps:

1. Outline the problem audience members are dealing with.
2. Describe both the current situation and the ideal situation.
3. Show that the current situation can be improved on.
4. Outline how your solution creates the ideal situation.
5. Show how adopting your solution will solve the problem.

Then make it simple for them to buy your solution/product/ service. Because of credit cards, it has never been easier for people to make instantaneous buying decisions, especially when they feel enthusiastic after your presentation. So when they do decide to buy, make sure they do so from you and they do it now.

The logic is quite simple. Why would people part with their money unless you're solving their problems or satisfying their perceived needs? The amount they spend is in proportion to three things: (1) their perception of the size of their problem, (2) the consequences of not taking action, and (3) the value of whatever solution they find.

Why do people spend money on luxury items when a basic item usually performs more than 90 percent of the required functions (for example, buying motor vehicles, TV sets, cell phones)? The answer is the same as above—that is, the more luxurious item satisfies their perceived need, even if that need is the desire to be seen as successful. Your ability to find an audience member's "hot button"—in this case, a need for a high-end product—is your key to their deciding in your favor.

The same principle applies in non-sales situations. For example, the young man who asks for his lady-love's hand in marriage needs to satisfy her father's desire to know that he'll keep her safe and happy.

CEOs need to convince employees who are implementing a new strategy that they'll overcome glitches in the production process (their problems), facilitate smoother operations (thus reduce their stress), and foster increased productivity and higher profits (bottom line).

Offer a value proposition that solves their problems and you'll get their buy-in.

Sales presentation—what is your competitive edge?

If two suppliers offered exactly the same product of exactly the same quality and color at exactly the same price and you could only choose one, which would you choose? Unless one supplier has an established relationship, many people choose neither—they simply keep looking until they find the right fit.

When given a choice, people select, often in a split second, what they perceive to benefit them most. In simple terms, they seek the "edge" that tips the scale on their decision-making—the "something" that's most important to them.

In a market saturated with great products at good prices, strong warranties, and lofty claims, the "edge" is what people want that they can't get elsewhere—newer, better, cleverer, more noticeable, higher value, and so on.

Today it's about capturing people's attention by being different. So before you plan your presentation, identify your edge—the one factor that makes you stand out from your competitors. Because if you don't have an edge, what do you have?

Not surprisingly, you'll find the same principle applies to selling an idea, a plan of action, or a viewpoint that encourages audience members to get involved or take action.

Did it deliver on your objective?

It's wonderful to pull off a slick presentation knowing everything went well: you finished on time, you made emotional connections, you felt people liked you. These are all good, but did you succeed in achieving these critical outcomes:

1. Did the audience understand what your central point was?

2. Did you clearly state your key objective?

3. Did you actually ask for the business?

4. Did your audience buy your product/service/idea?

Many seemingly good presentations actually fail to get the sale or persuade listeners to take the desired course of action. That's why it's critical to put a strong "outcomes strategy" in place before you start.

Put simply, at what stage will you ask people for your desired outcome and how will you close if they say yes? Preparing for your presentation using these important steps—begin with the end in mind—and you've set a clear objective.

KEY LESSONS FROM CHAPTER 3

1. You'll get exactly what you aim for, so set a clear objective from the start—begin with the end in mind.

2. A business presentation is an opportunity to convince people in the audience of your solution to their problem.

3. Having clarity of purpose saves you time and helps you structure your talk.

4. In determining your objective, ask yourself: "What do I want them to do afterward?"

5. For people who don't take action immediately, determine a strategy to follow up and remind them.

6. People assess your solution based on solving their problem. Make sure you've done your research and packed your solution (your value proposition) with benefits, not features.

7. If your objective is to sell a product/service/idea, identify your competitive edge and communicate it clearly.

8. Ask for a commitment or an agreement of intent when you close your presentation.

CHAPTER 4

PREPARING AND STRUCTURING CONTENT

"If I had eight hours to cut down a tree, I'd spend six hours sharpening
the axe."

—Former U.S. President Abraham Lincoln

Going in with a plan

Many years ago, I attended a course on selling and decided to
immediately put into action a key segment of what I had learned.
I had a big appointment coming up—a presentation to a human
resources director, a marketing manager, and four factory managers of a pharmaceutical company. They needed a program to
increase the hands-on leadership skills of their 40 supervisors in
charge of four production lines.

I started the presentation by providing a five-minute overview of my company, describing aspects of my operation that were relevant to the listeners. I then requested permission to ask them a few questions, to which they all agreed. I asked the first factory manager what he saw as the ideal outcome of the course for his people. He listed seven outcomes. I wrote them all down, repeated all seven back to him, and asked if I had them all correct. He nodded. I went to the next manager and did the same. He stated that he agreed with his previous colleague and added add two more points. I wrote them down and then read the list of nine points back to him. He nodded. The third manager only added one point. Again, I wrote it down, repeating all 10 points. He nodded. Then I addressed the fourth manager, who added two of his own and said that one of the previous points was not important to him.

I thanked him and then read all 12 points back to the group, making eye contact with all six participants. I was careful to say each manager's name when reading his points. I then asked the marketing manager, also by name, if he had anything to add. "No," he assured me, "I'd heard it all from the horse's mouth." The human resources director waved me on to continue.

Next, I briefly outlined the program that would meet their needs and how it worked, but I kept this to three minutes. Armed with their 12 desired outcomes, I then showed them, point by point, exactly how the program would meet these outcomes. This took about 25 minutes. More nodding of heads. Then I invited questions from them. I was asked three questions, mostly logistical, but nothing that came close to being an objection.

I ended by asking them when they'd like to see the process completed. I was told it would be within the next four months. I then promised them a proposal outlining what had been discussed.

In turn, they promised to answer me within a week of receiving the written proposal. I had my answer by the end of that week—a resounding yes and a request for dates.

Do you see how I had gone in knowing exactly what I would do and how I would do it? I was in control of the entire presentation and conducted it in a friendly, cooperative atmosphere. Within a short time, I had my desired outcome and the participants had theirs.

If you are serious about delivering a successful presentation, it's imperative to get organized early on in the planning stages and stay organized. When a presentation doesn't succeed, a lack of proper organization is often pinpointed as the main culprit.

Remember, being successful doesn't mean "getting through" the presentation; it means achieving the objective you set for it!

Unfortunately, this point eludes many presenters whose primary objective seems to be winning popular approval. It's like doubling over with laughter at a clever ad but not remembering the product it was advertising. Smart is good, but proper preparation ensures that any clever parts complement your main message and are only used in proper context.

Get highly organized

Put simply, human beings exist because billions of atoms and molecules have combined in particular ways to create exactly what we are. The combination of atoms is not random; it's highly organized in a specified order, much like the components of a fine building.

It can't be too difficult to erect a structure—I managed it at the age of eight with help from Lego®! But to put up an enduring building that's admired and valuable requires a great deal of precise planning in consultation with an architect and builder who have the exact skills needed for this purpose.

Because presentations tend to be much the same, to make a difference, you need to put a good deal of thought into how to build yours. Granted, good content is vitally important. But if two presentations have excellent content and one of them is structured in a compelling way while the other simply gushes forth without organization, which one is more likely to achieve the desired objective?

Make it matter

Without structure, your talk is merely matter, so put it together to make it matter. This requires preparation and preparation requires time.

The simplest presentation structure has three parts: a good Introduction (to be no more than 10 percent of your presentation), a substantial Body (to show the benefits of your value proposition) and a Conclusion (to sum up what you're proposing and convey a call to action)? Sounds dead simple, doesn't it? Let's examine each of these.

Introduction—"Telling 'em what you're gonna tell 'em"

For a business presentation, I suggest starting by targeting your message toward the audience you'll address. Ask: *Why would audience members come to listen to you? What's in it for them?* Answering these questions may require a little research, so first, phone the organizer or a secretary to find out the profile of the audience.

Find out how many will likely attend and how most people will dress. Also get information about the venue (for instance, what time you can have access to the venue or the stage, how the room will be set up, is there a PA system and microphone supplied—though I suggest always bringing your own anyway). Also check the organization's website to understand more about its business and purpose.

In the first few seconds of your presentation, audience members are compiling their first impression of you. Giving a strong, compelling opening statement ensures you'll set up the objective of your talk as soon as you open your mouth. If your opening statement is provocative or controversial, all the better—you'll immediately grab their attention. As soon as you complete your "headline opening statement," then introduce what you intend to talk about during the rest of your presentation. (Please don't confuse Introduction in this context with your introduction by your host as the presenter. Chapter 12 addresses that kind of introduction.)

The Body—"Tell 'em!"

In the Body of a business presentation, your compelling argument is designed to persuade your audience to see certain information your way. One effective way to accomplish this is to appear objective by explaining two or three options. As noted in Chapter 3, you could begin by stating the current situation, and then outlining the options.

For example, one option may be for the organization to stay the same until the new technology is available. A second option would be to make a few inexpensive adjustments to tide everyone over until the new technology is on stream. A third option would be to upgrade immediately using current technology.

Next, you'd describe some benefits and downfalls of the two options you don't recommend. This indicates your objectivity. Then you'd present the option you consider the best solution and persuasively (but not aggressively!) outline all of its key benefits. You may also wish to highlight a few downside consequences of not taking action on your recommendations. Of course, you don't want to appear preachy; you're simply "persuasively enlightening" your listeners. Always keep in mind that people love buying but they hate being sold to; you don't ever want them to feel manipulated.

Question Time *Before* The End

Before heading toward the Conclusion, something important awaits—Question Time. Beware. Question Time can be the death of many a presentation, mainly for two reasons: (1) The presenter positions it at the end of the presentation, the disadvantage being that the presentation may lack a firm, results-oriented conclusion. But a more disastrous potential pitfall is this: If question time goes wrong, the result is that the presentation concludes on a negative note and/or (2) the presenter gets drawn into an argument with a questioner who disagrees, resulting in the presenter becoming defensive. As soon as this happens, credibility is lost and doubt is sown in the minds of your listeners. I recommend acknowledging a viewpoint that differs from yours without arguing.

It's best to end by delivering a strong summary in the Conclusion, which should follow Question Time, not precede it. Good protocol is to repeat each question in summary form so everyone can hear it and give yourself a few extra seconds to formulate your reply. (Read more about how to handle Question Time in Chapter 10.)

Conclusion—"Tell 'em what you told 'em"

The Conclusion, which takes between 6 and 15 percent of your presentation time, is when you deliver your final call to action. Do this by concisely but clearly repeating the main points from the Body, touching on all options but focusing on your solution and its benefits, and then requesting action. Do you see how positioning Question Time before the Conclusion allows you to close on a positive and compelling note?

Numerous studies about prospective buyers who failed to take the bait indicate the number one reason for a "no-buy decision" was the salesperson's failure to ask for the business! After all the trouble you've taken preparing and delivering a great presentation, don't let this be your most grievous sin!

Clive Simpkins, an accomplished professional speaker who's coached presenters for decades, has this to say about structuring presentations:

When it comes to organizing content, think of it like a wagon wheel. The hub is your objective and the answer to the question: "What do I want to happen in their minds when I've left the room?" The spokes are the content elements. They're there because they help you deliver on the objective. They don't get included unless they move you toward accomplishment of that objective. The rim represents the complete circle of attitude, perception, and behavioral shifts that you'll get as a result of using an objectives-based approach.

Content needs to have a thread of continuity. Corny though it may sound, I liken it to a necklace. Though sometimes invisible, there's nevertheless a thread running through the beads of the necklace. The factual elements are the beads along the thread of your presentation. In between, you add little anecdotes, quotations, evidence, examples, your experience, or items of interest to add sparkle and maintain attention spans—which, today, are notoriously short! These are the entertainment elements.

If yours is a good presentation or talk, it'll satisfy the PIE acronym requirements. Persuade, Inform, and Edu-tain (Educate-Entertain). Then what you say will be memorable and result in a call to action.

Never forget that presenting or communicating is theatre. Some of it is serious, some light-hearted, some even farcical. You decide on the positioning, but think like a producer or theatre director. As the Western world doyen of advertising David Ogilvy famously said, "You can't bore your clients into buying your product or service!" Make it fun.

—Clive Simpkins, change architect,
strategist and author of *The Concise Communicator*
www.clivesimpkins.com

Structure in non-business presentations

Sometimes presentations—like an inspirational or a business-topic keynote—are delivered with soft outcomes in mind. Still, using structure in these talks is every bit as important. You need an Introduction and Body followed by a Conclusion. But you might "blend" the talk more throughout and, instead of having a concrete call for action at the end, deliver an impactful closing statement.

As you gain experience, you'll learn to deliver your talks more and more spontaneously. This all comes with practice, increased confidence, and more familiarity with the subject.

Stick to your allocated time

Most presentations or talks are scheduled for a specific amount of time. Please pay careful attention to these five important reasons why you should stick to your time slot:

1. Your audience is geared for a certain amount of time; listeners do have lives outside of hearing you speak.
2. Other speakers who have a limited allocated time may be following your talk.
3. Caterers can't keep food warm indefinitely.
4. The venue may be booked for a limited period only.
5. The most important reason is this: The shorter and more compact your talk, the more impact it will have.

Your best method of ensuring that your presentation can be delivered within set time limits is to practice it a lot, doing dry runs without interruptions. Chapter 5 provides an in-depth description of this important part of your preparation—the rehearsal.

Staying on track

You can use cue cards to stay on track with both the structure of your talk and its timing. This is particularly valuable when creating a new presentation. See Chapter 2 for ways to use them. You'll find cue cards dealt with from a different perspective in Chapter 6.

KEY LESSONS FROM CHAPTER 4

1. Organizing your presentation properly is vital in achieving your intended outcomes.

2. In your presentation, select the information your audience needs most to react to your call to action. They seldom need much.

3. Structure involves an Introduction, Body, and Conclusion, with the Body taking up the lion's share of the allocated time.

4. Practice your presentation so you can complete it in the allocated time without rushing.

5. Decide whether you will allow questions during the presentation. If you want to have them, factor in some time after the Body but before the Conclusion.

6. Cue cards can be used to help you to stay on track.

CHAPTER FIVE
PRACTICING—
THE MISSING INGREDIENT

"It usually takes me more than three weeks to prepare a good impromptu speech."

—American writer Mark Twain

Why most people fail to rehearse

There are several reasons. It's likely that, in most cases, more than one of these apply:

1. Not understanding the multifaceted value of practice
2. Not making the time to practice (they usually say they didn't have the time!)
3. Thinking that preparation involves only structuring material

4. Spending all one's preparation time preparing a slideshow

5. Setting aside the time but becoming distracted—in other words, failing to prioritize

6. Just plain laziness

One can compare learning to speak publicly with learning to drive a car. When you get behind the wheel for the first time, you soon realize you don't have the *skills* to drive, regardless of how much theoretical study you've done or how much you've watched your parents. Fortunately, you understand you can learn the skills you need, so you eagerly go about learning them and practicing your driving. Finally, you take your driver's test and, if you pass, you're rewarded by receiving your driver's license. You do this so you won't be a hazard to yourself and others, or be fined for not having a license.

Now, you won't be fined for presenting a speech without having a license—there's no law against it anywhere in the world. But if I could have my way, one day a license will be required!

When you put together and deliver your first presentation, you may not be surprised that there's more to it than may have initially passed through your mind. If your first presentation is already behind you, you will know exactly what I mean—especially if the intended outcome was completely missed. After a first shattering experience, you might decide you're simply not cut out for presenting. I suggest saying to yourself something like this: "I can't present competently yet, but with some practice, I'll get there!"

The keyword is practice.

After I gave my first presentation skills course, I was elated. I felt I'd come out of it well and had acquired the tools to make really good presentations. Only one problem: I was really like that beginning driver with a new license—that is, lots of enthusiasm and practically no experience. Initially my presentation "hit rate" did not seem to be improving at all. In one instance, I found that in correcting certain weaknesses, my focus shifted away from things I'd previously done well. At first it was frustrating; I felt I was getting worse, not better. I later discovered that it often goes like that.

In learning any skill, we often go through a few rough patches until it all starts pulling together. The principle that proved to be of most value here was perseverance. Ultimately, gaining gradual experience proved most decisive.

So it is with so many presentation skills graduates—lots of practical tools, no real experience yet. And for those who don't use all the tools explained in this book, that's how it stays. Some presenters create opportunities to practice these exciting new skills while others don't. Dangerously, they delude themselves that they know what to do because they've completed a course. However, to *know* how to do something and to *be able to do it* is like the difference between the equator and the South Pole.

Practice runs

In my presentation skills training, I've identified two distinct categories of practice: practice runs and ongoing practice. Let's deal with practice runs first. This is the category I refer to when I use the phrase "the missing ingredient." It's the part of the presentation process that's most often neglected, usually with disastrous results.

You might deliver your practice run of a new presentation in front of a mirror, using a camcorder, or talking to a "soft" audience like a colleague or family member. This allows you to familiarize yourself with your flow and check if it works. But doing only one dry run is seldom enough because you'll find yourself making many necessary adjustments during this initial attempt. It rarely runs smoothly. Your first run checks the flow of your presentation and allows you to tidy it up. Your second dry run is often spectacularly better and this surprises most people. It shouldn't. By now, you know what you want to say. Consider the second run to be your real practice. Many presenters need no more than two practice runs to be ready, but some require a third "for insurance."

It's also important to rehearse if you'll be giving the same presentation for a new audience, especially if it's a different type of audience. Make any necessary adjustments to your presentation, then rehearse the changes. If you have no changes, do a practice run anyway, especially if some time has elapsed since your previous presentations.

Ongoing practice

The second category involves ongoing practice, which is practicing your skills by presenting frequently. Unfortunately, many presenters gain live experience without first being trained and develop habits that can prove problematic later. It's like building a house without a proper foundation.

Beware. Experience gained without learning proper skills up front can be a hit-and-miss affair. You run the same risk as the self-taught driver does—that is, you can drive but you lack essential skills and knowledge. On the other hand, those who do not apply the theory they've learned soon after being exposed to it see the information dissipate or fade away. This makes recalling it increasingly difficult as time progresses. With the information overload we experience today, our brains quickly disperse what we don't use, so it becomes a matter of "use it or lose it." That's why it's essential for you to apply the new information very soon after completing the training.

Discipline

Many cite lack of time as the reason they don't practice. Let me put it to you this way: It has little to do with actual time and everything to do with discipline and preparation. After all, everyone has the same amount of time available each day—24 hours. It's your choice whether you place enough importance on your presentation to plan your time frames properly. If you deem your presentation important enough, then factor in sufficient time to rehearse the flow through your practice runs. The ideal planning scenario is to complete your structure and slides three days ahead of your actual presentation. That gives you one evening and an additional two days to fit in the practice time you need.

Another reason presenters might feel nervous is because they haven't thoroughly tested their presentation. Remember, it's only untested if you've never done it before. The best way to get past this is by rehearsing in front of that most forgiving but most honest of friends—your dear mirror. Doing that lets you test your timing (not on the first run, but on the second!). When you get it right, your confidence in the effectiveness of your flow will increase and your nervousness will disappear.

Here's the trick: when your scheduled practice time arrives, start rehearsing whether you feel ready or not. Add this dimension to your preparation and the rest will fall in place faster anyway. As you review your performances from that point forward, you're likely to see and feel improvement and an associated increase in confidence— the real reward for your efforts, courage, and discipline. And, believe me, all three are required to turn out a decent speech!

Alan Stevens, a presentation skills coach and established international speaker, has this to say about rehearsing your presentation:

South African golfing legend Gary Player is credited with coining this phrase: "The more I practice, the luckier I get." This came in response to a bystander's comment of "lucky" after Player had holed the 17th in one stroke. Like most aphorisms, it's essentially true. Most of us resist practice, whether it's a musical instrument, a sport, or a foreign language. Yet the best exponents of any discipline are those who work hard at honing their skills.

Why don't people practice before they speak? In some cases, it's because they think they are a "natural speaker." There may be something in that, but I've seen some of the greatest "natural speakers" groping for words or becoming tongue-tied. Others believe they'll lose spontaneity if they practice too much. There is some truth in that because over-rehearsal can make you sound stilted and robotic. However, the impact on your audience of under-rehearsal is much worse than it is for over-rehearsal.

No actor would dream of appearing in a play without rehearsing. When you speak to your audiences, therefore, you should pay them the same respect as being an actor putting on a performance. When you rehearse, it allows you to make sure your timing is right, and that you feel comfortable in the outfit you plan to wear (you see, even speakers need a dress rehearsal). If you need to use props or slides, it helps you fit them seamlessly into your presentation.

An effective way to practice (although members of my family may disagree) is to perform to a live audience, however small. Most important, ask for feedback, listen to it, and act on it if necessary. That way, you'll become a very "lucky" speaker indeed. And who couldn't do with a bit of "luck" every now and then?

—Alan Stevens, author of *The Media Coach*
www.mediacoach.com

Rehearsing helps your presentation flow

Rehearsal is not intended to create a word-perfect presentation, which may sound stiff and unconvincing. The purpose of practice is to create familiarity with the flow and the way you have structured your presentation. Getting familiar with what you've planned to tell your audience ensures that you tell them only what they need to know to evoke a decision. You have your background knowledge of your subject to fall back on if questions arise.

Rehearsal is the most important differentiation between success and failure on the day. Practice is, indeed, the missing ingredient!

Although this chapter is among the shortest, it's the most important for many. Remember, the difference between successful and unsuccessful people is that the former are prepared to do the things the latter won't do.

The stuff of champions

At the time of this writing, most would agree that Pete Sampras is the most accomplished male tennis player of all time. With a record 14 Grand Slam titles, few before or after him have accomplished what he did with the same consistency. How did he manage to dominate so convincingly at a time when the modern game had become so ultra-competitive?

Despite winning more matches than any other player on the professional circuit (thus compelling him to spend more match-time on court than the others), Sampras was known to still absorb as much coaching time as the other top players. Most people take a few lessons, believe they've "got it," and quit the lessons. But the world's number one tennis champ spent more time on court on a weekly basis than his main competitors. While watching a TV documentary on Sampras, I was fascinated to learn that Pete won a higher percentage of points on his second serve than any other player in the game—something that takes considerable practice to accomplish consistently. You only achieve these kinds of results through unwavering confidence, which in turn comes from an accumulation of experience.

Pete's success in this important area of his game says something about the value of practicing your craft, wouldn't you say?

> "It is worth noting that an amateur practices until she gets it right;
>   a professional practices until she can't get it wrong."
>
> —Anonymous

KEY LESSONS FROM CHAPTER 5

1. Practice is the least glamorous part of presenting, but it's your bridge between failure and success.

2. Two good practice runs are 30 times more valuable to your presentation than getting your last three slides right.

3. If you wait until you're ready, you'll never start practicing. Schedule your practice date and time, and always start on time.

4. If you're an expert on the subject of your presentation, two to three practice runs should be sufficient to become comfortable with the flow of your talk.

5. Experiencing pre-presentation nerves has little to do with ability and everything to do with familiarity with your planned flow. With familiarity comes confidence. With confidence comes a good presentation.

6. Preparing the flow comes first, then getting comfortable with it. This is only attained through practice.

7. The term "luck" in the context of presentations is a synonym for the word "rehearse."

8. Understanding the value of this crucial step separates successful presenters from unsuccessful ones.

9. Depending on your objective of a particular practice run, you can rehearse in front of a friendly audience, a camcorder, or a mirror.

10. If you're doing the same presentation for a different audience, rehearse again.

CHAPTER 6
VISUAL IMPACT—YOU

"And since you know you cannot see yourself so well as by reflection, I,
your glass, will modestly discover to yourself that of yourself which you
yet know not of."

—Poet and playwright William Shakespeare

Initial impact

Based on a well-publicized adage, you have around seven seconds
to make a first impression. Whether it's really five or even 13 seconds isn't that important. Point is, it's so brief that no one should
have trouble holding one's breath that long.

This initial impression is likely to linger more powerfully than
anything you do afterward. It gets your audience with you from
the start, making it much easier to keep them with you for the
duration of your presentation.

And that doesn't refer to what you say. Although your opening words make up a vital part of your entrance, the audience *sees* you before they *hear* you. Your overall visual appearance creates expectation and supports your message. In some instances, your audiences may already be familiar with your brand, having seen your promotional materials in advance.

How you dress is a significant part of the first impression and so is how you move. Do you appear confident or hesitant? Does everything about your appearance "fit" or are you wearing or doing something that would distract people? Smiling adds enormously to the overall package you're presenting; only avoid smiling when it's inappropriate. Brand image specialist and professional speaker **Lesley Everett** offers this advice on creating your personal image and brand:

Projecting our brand comes in many forms—from the quality of our voice, our body indicators, our behavior and attitude, and, of course, the way we dress. Whether we like it or not, people do judge us on the way we dress. Over the past 13 years of developing and evolving my methodology, I have experienced the remarkably significant amount of emphasis we put, subconsciously, on this element of other people's brands and the impact they make in business. We just can't get away from it so we'd be well advised to take control of the way we dress and our non-verbal communication generally; it does form a powerful part of the overall message we project.

It's no good talking about the high quality of your products, for example, if you look tired, your clothes are dated and ill-fitted, and your grooming leaves a lot to be desired! Certainly on a first impression, audience members believe what they see rather than what they hear.

Over the years, many times a company has called me to work with its employees as "they don't project the corporate brand well and the image of the company is being diluted."

With "business casual" dress becoming the norm in today's global business world, more relaxed dress can be adopted for some business presentations. This is where a lot of professionals dilute their personal brands! Remember, "business casual" does not mean you can relax the professional image you project—it's not a "licensed slob" day!

It is possible to still project a cutting-edge image and create instant positive impact wearing casual clothes. You just have to bear in mind the following rules:

1. Apply the same criteria to your business casual wardrobe as you would to your sharpest suited look—for example, does it fit well, is it still up to date, is it past its best, does it have marks on it that you think nobody will notice (they always do, by the way!)?

2. Take into account—
   - The makeup of the audience and its expectations of you and your company
   - The environment and the situation
   - Your own objectives

If you consider all of these, you'll come up with the most appropriate outfit.

Your image when presenting is as important as your content because without a congruent, non-verbal message, your key content will never be as impactful as you need it to be.

And always remember, when you're presenting, your image gets magnified when the audience members' eyes rest on you!

—Lesley Everett, author of *Drop Dead Brilliant*
www.lesleyeverett.com

Your attire—what to wear

When you arrive appropriately attired, you place yourself at ease and focus on your setup and what you're going to say.

Choices regarding presentation attire can be contentious because of shifting trends toward informal dress. Some folks get particularly hot under the collar about it. Unfortunately, with the rapid demise of the quality of major spoken languages (including English), far too many people interpret "informal" to mean "sloppy." They pay for it dearly when they dress improperly for a formal presentation.

Your selection of attire for a presentation will go a long way toward making you feel at ease at the start. But what attire is correct? This depends on where you're presenting (city or country) and whom you're presenting to. What is the nature of their business? What is their culture and corporate dress code? Is your topic light-hearted or serious?

Do your homework! The time-honored presentation rule may be your best guide. It says try to establish how the majority of audience members will dress, and then dress one step up or at least the same. Dressing down from your audience affects your credibility. Being dressed the same creates mutual comfort and is good for information-sharing-style presentations. One step up gives you added authority and enhanced credibility—an important element in being persuasive. However, if the dress gap is too severe, you can create trouble for yourself. For example, if you're too dressed up, they may feel intimidated and will not warm to you. If you dress down too much, your audience may think you lack respect.

It is also wise to align your attire with your message. For example, those advising others about their finances would be expected to wear a business suit to establish credibility. But if you're addressing the shop floor staff about a new pension fund, a more casual approach like wearing a blazer with an open-neck shirt is likely to put your audience at ease.

The rule of thumb is this: Consider which outfit will optimize your chances of success. Then check it out in the mirror. If it *looks* bad, it *is* bad. Put yourself in their shoes (theoretically, of course!) and if you think you'd buy from this person, then you've made a good choice.

The age-old rule for presentation attire—dressing one step up, or similar to, the level that you expect of your audience—can prove to be an over simplistic approach. Often, audience members may arrive in mixed levels of attire. In this case, select your dress at the level of the expected smartest-dressed attendee. However, casual attire can be appropriate for smaller groups, for when a great deal of interaction is expected with the audience and for when equipment is being demonstrated.

Darker colors like navy, charcoal, and black—power colors—work well when presenting to large audiences (especially when compared with a white or cream shirt or blouse). The V created by a suit centers eyes on your upper chest and head. This effect gets highlighted when you wear a contrasting tie or scarf.

Avoid wearing bulky clothing; you want to look trim and neat. Remove any items that may bulge, like wallets or purses, cigarettes, keys, handkerchiefs, or tissues.

A word of caution: If you lose a button or dip a corner of your jacket in a cheese dip by accident, have it repaired or cleaned as soon as you get home. If you don't, you're bound to forget about it. When you're getting ready, having to sew on a button is the last thing you want to do—especially when you're "playing an away game."

Wear dark shoes

Black is the best color for shoes during a presentation; *polished* is the best condition. The more formal the presentation, the more important it is that you choose black, or at least dark shoes—without white socks, that is! For gents, match your sock color with your trousers, not your shirt, and make sure your belt is also black to match your shoes. Consider these your safe, conservative "default settings."

However, our changing world may favor dressing in a more daring way. Image specialist **Haydee Antezana** advises that when presenting, you take more time and effort into "looking the part" than you would for your normal morning routine.

To increase your confidence and reduce your stress when presenting, she offers these image tips:

- Rather overdress than underdress; better to be conservative than too trendy.

- Make sure your outfit is comfortable. You have enough to worry about without wincing because your new shoes are too tight.
- Choose simple styles in exceptional quality fabrics.
- Do not wear anything that can distract from your message (e.g., bold patterns, prints, loud accessories, too many bright colors, etc.).
- Clothes must hang well, allow you to move effortlessly, and be wrinkle free.
- Find out the color of the background you'll be speaking against. A black suit against a black curtain will make you appear like you have a disembodied head.
- An accent color anchored by neutral colors (e.g., an orange shirt with a black suit) always makes an impact.
- Wear lighter neutral colors in summer: beige, stone, grey. Darker neutrals work better in winter: chocolate, charcoal, navy.
- A small amount of red in a shirt or a tie gives the impression of being confident, knowledgeable, and decisive. Wearing too much black may convey that you're not open to negotiation and you are too serious. Blue tones depict trustworthiness and loyalty.
- If befitting the company dress code, wear a jacket. It will provide you with more credibility and hide a multitude of sins. Ensure it buttons properly and fits you correctly.
- Impeccable grooming, clean nails, and subtle fragrance and makeup are essential for a complete look of excellence.
- Ensure that your glasses are non-reflective. Remove them if necessary.

- Follow the "4 A" guidelines for the Ideal Presentation Outfit:
    1. Assured—Does it make me feel confident and assured?
    2. Appropriate—Is it company, location, industry appropriate?
    3. Attractive—Does it fit me correctly? Do I look good in it?
    4. Accessories—Do my accessories enhance or distract from my message?

"If you do not believe the messenger, you will not believe the message."—Anonymous

—Haydee Antezana, CEO of Professional Impressions
www.profimpressions.co.za

Your body language

Of our five senses, we rely predominantly on our eyes for information. Research reveals that the eyes give sighted people as much as 87 percent of their information. This further supports the notion that the visual information we present has an overriding impact on the success of any presentation, particularly at the start.

It is common for unskilled presenters to focus their preparation on content without reviewing the visual aspects of the presentation adequately—apart from the slideshow. What about your own body? What messages are your eyes, arms, legs, and torso giving to your audience? If you haven't been videoed doing a presentation lately (or don't practice your talks in front of a mirror), you may not be aware of what these combined components—your body language—are telling your audiences. In terms of initial impact, body language gives more information than anything else. The content—the words and ideas themselves—often have a limited initial impact, building as the presentation goes on. What's more influential in creating likeability and credibility is the tone of your voice.

Think of it this way: The message seldom unfolds in the first few seconds. It usually takes at least three to five minutes, if not longer. A skilled presenter can overcome this with a powerful opening statement. But audiences are impatient; people tend to subconsciously decide within the first ten seconds if they like what they see. Then, once they get used to what you're wearing, their attention will shift away from your attire, but the initial impression will likely remain. Although your tone of voice remains a key influencer, the power of your message gains prominence only as the presentation wears on.

Your movement

In my experience as a presentation skills facilitator, I've noticed that one of the most common pitfalls of presenters, experienced or not, is their fidgeting. If they do it enough, their audiences lose track of the message because they're anticipating the next antic. This results in losing credibility. How can your message be any good if you look suspect?

When you're doing a presentation, what looks best—walking around or standing still? The answer lies somewhere in between. Fidgeting while standing indicates you're nervous and so does pacing. Rocking and swaying may appear comical and also indicate nervousness. So when you decide to stand still, plant yourself on the ground and simply stand still. If, however, you want to move, do so slowly and purposefully. Move to where you're going, then "plant" yourself again. This shows you're in control. A combination of both techniques will make you appear most relaxed, especially if you have a wide stage. Actively use the stage to connect with the different sections of your audience. Also take a forward step or two to emphasize a point. If you do step back, do so during a pause. Remember, turning your back on the audience is taboo as it breaks eye contact and appears uncaring.

Your posture

Your stance or posture gives audience members subliminal information about how you feel about yourself and helps them settle on their first impression of you. This is where the mirror becomes your friend, for you can instantly see whether you are stooping, looking unbalanced, or standing upright. Clive Simpkins suggests thinking of it this way: "If your ears are dripping, the drops should fall on your shoulders, not your shoes." Doesn't that sum it up nicely?

Naturally, you want to look human, not stiff, and relaxed, not tense. Your upright, confident, relaxed posture supports the impression of relaxed confidence that you want to convey.

To gesture or not to gesture

How do gestures fit in to the picture?

This is best answered by considering the alternatives to gesturing. A presenter using a lectern needs to make maximum impact with her voice. A presenter without a lectern who shows her whole body looks robotic if she stands still and doesn't use gestures. On the other hand, leaping about and gesticulating wildly looks comical.

People best show their natural ability to gesticulate appropriately when they're in a spontaneous animated conversation. If they can be recorded doing this, it should be easy to teach them to re-enact these gestures in a formal presentation environment.

One extremely distracting thing to watch for is waving your hands in front of you repetitively—something people often do when they feel nervous. In contrast, polished speakers use gestures skillfully to emphasize key points. They also mix their gestures so they're not repetitive. When combined with a few slow, deliberate steps, the speaker looks confident and in control, creating an impression of being a credible person.

Avoid putting your hands behind your back—often done during question time, as it suggests you're hiding something from your audience and that you are not being entirely honest. Hands in pockets is also not advised, although for lengthy presentations in an informal setting, it can make you appear relaxed and personable. Any hand-to-face gestures can be seen as signs of uncertainly and may also be interpreted as dishonesty.

Presenters who clasp their hands in front of them below the waist in a fig leaf position are seen as defensive and are less likely to be trusted. The same goes for the wrist lock, lower arm lock, elbow lock, upper arm lock, and folded arms. Presenters often adopt these positions to keep their hands occupied as many people are at a loss with what to do with their hands when on stage. They don't intend to send a defensive message; they just want to control their hands.

As uncomfortable as it may initially feel, hands that are not occupied by gesturing or holding cue cards should be left neatly at your side with palms facing the legs. It feels strange at first, but it looks good, and gradually you'll become used to it! However, if this still seems awkward, clasp the palm of one hand by the thumb and index finger of the other hand. This somehow looks relaxed and doesn't convey a closed position. Just remember to disengage yourself when it's time to use a big, bold gesture to help you drive home an important point.

Your feedback mechanism

How do you ensure you get everything right on the day of your presentation? You look at yourself before you go "live." Trust me on this one. Confident body language sets you up to competently deliver your content. Your easiest option is to practice in front of a mirror, which lets you see how your audience will see you and gives you a chance to iron out mannerisms that might be distracting.

Your other option is to use a camcorder, mount it on a tripod, and videotape your presentation (or the part you wish to review and play it back), critically reviewing the areas that need improving. You can rewind where necessary to focus on key areas and correct the irritators that could turn people off.

Using these aids, experiment by mixing your gestures, seeing how they come across, and deciding what works best. You can also choreograph certain gestures to increase the impact at certain key points in your presentation. Make sure you allocate enough time for rehearsing the body language aspect of your presentation—the part that strongly affects the impression you leave.

Using cue cards

A previous chapter addressed using cue cards during a presentation. If you've witnessed speakers presenting while clutching a large sheet of paper or a notepad, you'd agree this appears unprofessional. Cue cards or index cards work better.

Be aware, however, that holding cue cards engage a hand that could be used for effective gesturing. Never wave cue cards about as this looks downright silly. If you have a remote control device in the other hand, your options are further limited. You could place your cue cards on an easily accessible table or lectern, but you want to access them quickly without upsetting your rhythm—another reason you need to practice in advance.

Hold your cue cards easily in your hand, not too high up, just slightly above belt level. Hold them in the palm of your hand or by the corner. If you wish to gesture, do so with the hand that isn't holding the cards. You can also transfer the cards to your other hand.

Please avoid spending most of your presentation burying your nose in your cue cards! The trick is to speak *to* your audience, not *at* them. Simply glance at the card, look up, and then speak. As you end one point, glance at the card again to pick up your next point, look up and pause simultaneously, then start your next point. Make sure any changeover is seamless and not dramatic. As one of the world's best-loved voice coaches, Betty Cooper from Calgary, Canada, advises: "When your mouth is open, your eyes are up." Remember it.

Use of a lectern

A lectern is a barrier that hides many a sin. One associates lecterns with lecturers, old-style church pastors, and company officers presenting financial results. The main purpose of the lectern, of course, is to provide a place for notes. It's particularly useful in a dark venue because it has a reading light. But when you hide your body behind it and bury your eyes in your notes, you markedly diminish your persuasive powers!

Although many presenters who use lecterns are vocally skilled, they can improve their performance substantially by moving away from it and using body language effectively. I saw this myself when I attended a presentation by relationship expert Jackie Black. She spent the first hour behind the lectern and, although her content was good, my attention strayed for most of that hour. Then she stepped out from behind the lectern and started speaking more directly to the audience. After a time, she took questions. For me, her presentation changed the instant she left the lectern behind. She had me mesmerized right through to the end.

The Best Shortcut to Presentation Success
Study a true speaking professional in action. Hey, the wheel was invented ages ago. No point trying to reinvent it. Besides, who has the time?

KEY LESSONS FROM CHAPTER 6

1. People gain their initial impression from your visual appearance—your attire and body language—and this stays with them.

2. As your presentation progresses, the impact of your content should increase until it becomes the dominant factor.

3. Make your movements slow and deliberate; this indicates confidence and credibility.

4. Use bold gestures to enhance your key points. Be aware that repetitive gestures or flapping about will detract from your message.

5. Use one of the following four feedback mechanisms to improve the visual aspects of your presentation: live audience, camcorder, digital recorder, or mirror.

6. Use cue cards as notes if necessary. Avoid putting notes on 8½ X 11 sheets of paper; they make you appear unprepared. If you have a full set of notes, place them on the lectern provided.

7. If you're not in control of your body language, your content and vocal skills need to be excellent to get you back into stride.

8. Keep your attire appropriate to the nature of the presentation you're delivering. The standard rule is to dress similarly to your audience or one step up. Wear clothing that helps you feel comfortable and confident that you look your best.

9. Use a lectern if you need to refer to notes extensively. However, you'll have more impact if you move away from the lectern and maintain eye contact with your audience.

CHAPTER 7
VISUAL IMPACT—DATA PROJECTION

"You can have brilliant ideas, but if you can't get them across, your ideas won't get you anywhere."

—American industrialist Lee Iacocca

Why use a slide show?

The right picture is worth a thousand words. This is because visual information has far more power than information received by all the other senses combined. When you use the right kind of pictures, charts, and graphics, you can significantly improve the quality of your presentations. However, pictures used incorrectly can cause more harm than good.

The purpose of most presentations is to convince your audience of your point of view. Achieving this requires that you first ensure they remember what you say. This is one of the biggest advantages of using a slide show: the visuals create the powerful combination of hearing and seeing to help the audience to remember your words. This is particularly relevant when addressing an audience whose mother tongue is different from yours. They will rely on your slides for clarity on points that didn't quite gel when you said them.

The faithful old overhead projector was the tool used for presenter visuals until the turn of the decade, using overhead transparencies that could be created with a computer and printer. For high resolution combined with quick changeover, 35mm slides were also an option—but would take time to create as they would have to be professionally made up. This would make flexibility difficult. These mediums have, however, has been replaced by the laptop computer/data projector combination, which potentially could solve most projection problems. By 2005, with laptops and data projectors plummeting in price, overhead projectors had, in fact, become practically obsolete. We can therefore confine our focus to PowerPoint-style presentations and, to a lesser extent, video.

PowerPoint technology has effectively eradicated the major challenge presenters had with overhead projectors—managing their transparencies efficiently and making transitions* as smooth as possible. The physical changeover of transparencies has been replaced by the click of a remote button far away from the projector itself. But as we will discover, this seemingly easy, modern alternative has produced a fresh set of problems, the vast majority of them user-related.

*A transition refers to the changeover between slides. There are a number of options, such as fading between slides, the last slide exiting in any direction you choose to reveal the next one, and so on. In PowerPoint, if you click on Slide

Show on the menu bar and then Transitions, you will see a choice of available transitions.

Professional quality essential

Many take the decision to use slides lightly. They shouldn't because with this choice comes the obligation to put together a slide show that's professional and compelling. In reality, it is far better to have no slides than substandard ones. I can't emphasize strongly enough that you should learn to create excellent slides and professional-looking transitions, then practice your presentation with your slides so you know that your slide show will run seamlessly on presentation day.

Not every kind of slide show requires visuals; for instance, a one-on-one presentation seldom requires a slide show. So the first question is, "Do I really need a slide show and, if so, why?" If you have a good reason such as displaying graphs that could visually create clearer comparisons or you would like to describe aspects of a flow chart, then by all means go ahead. Another possibility is that you might want to build a compelling argument using bullet points to list key benefits. Be warned, however, that creating a slide show can be time consuming, contains many potential pitfalls, and can reveal you as an amateur if you don't learn to use the technology properly.

By far the majority of presenters, including professionals who speak for a living, create ineffective slide shows that detract from their message. I don't see this changing anytime soon, so there is an upside. If you use a slide show, the ineffectiveness of others by comparison gives you an advantage. So by all means use one, but if you do and you aren't yet a PowerPoint expert, become one. It takes time, but most people enjoy this learning curve and feel a sense of accomplishment when they've turned out a professional-looking show.

Simplicity

With the exception of speakers who deliver their presentations without slides as a keynoter may do, it's unusual for presenters not to spend a significant amount of time preparing their slide shows. Multimedia presentations are the "in thing" these days. There are so many things you can do to enhance the quality and effectiveness of your presentation. You can add music or video clips that cue automatically or with a mouse click; you can use different transitions to create required effects; you can set up a visual and musical theme that makes your presentation stronger. Indeed, a well-positioned piece of video or music can add flavor to your presentation, make it memorable, and help to drive your point home.

When you review your draft slide show, be courageous. Don't ever get so attached to a snippet of visual art that you lose track of the possibility it may do nothing to get your main message across. Two options then remain: change it or scrap it. As brutal as it may sound, the latter usually works best.

PowerPoint courses

Many people learn best by tinkering rather than taking a course and then trying to apply everything taught. In most cases, I advocate doing a combination of these. Tinker until you understand the basics of the program, then take a course—either online or in a classroom—to fast track yourself to presenting your information professionally.

These basic rules will serve you well to start with:

1. Slides are best used to illustrate key points. Any slide that does not is not required. In essence, use as few slides as possible. That way, the slides you do use will have greater impact.

2. Use a neutral background that blends in well with your theme. Busy or very bright backgrounds can give an aggressive undertone to your visuals that detracts from your message.

3. If you're going to use transitions, stick to one standard slide transition rather than using different ones throughout. This option is easier on the eyes and comes across more professionally.

4. Based on an increasing body of research, the current trend is to use as little text as possible on a slide—no more than a few words.

5. Use a cue system so that you know which slide comes next; reading off your monitor shows that you're not sure what is coming next. If you turn to look at the screen for your cue, you lose contact with your audience, which is even worse. So use each slide to emphasize your point, not introduce it.

6. If you're finished making a point using a visual, switch the visual off or people will look at the screen instead of at you. (If your remote mouse does not offer this function, use the "B" key on your keyboard.)

7. PowerPoint gives you the choice to animate or build the content of a slide rather than leave it static. To do this, it's best to bring up new slides with the heading already in place rather than having to use an additional slide to bring up the next element of the content. You simply add other elements to each slide as you speak about it by clicking the mouse. You can set it up to build elements automatically, but I don't recommend doing it this way because the automation can interfere with the pace of your speech.

8. Detailed slides are good for written reports and summary documents, but not for business-related presentations. If it's necessary to use a detailed technical slide, follow it with a simple, clear summary slide, never with another cluttered one. Simplify any slides that look cluttered.

9. You can save different versions of the same slide show for different target audiences. Make sure you file each slide show in the folder reserved for that topic and clearly mark each one. This way you can place a shortcut on your desktop the night before for the one you intend using the next day. Even then, always check that you've opened the right one.

10. Always carry a back-up slide show on a removable flash drive or CD and keep it separate from your laptop. (You'll read more about backup in Chapter 12.)

11. Laser pointers are useful when used correctly and are preferable to pointing to the screen with your arm, hand, or finger. "Correctly" means sparingly and not in an obvious manner. Refrain from waggling the laser or jabbing it toward the screen each time you use it. If you bear in mind that your audience has the ability to follow what's on the

screen, the laser pointer should rarely be necessary except to emphasize or repeat a previous point.

Not sure whether or not to use a slide show? You're deciding between applying for a position as a PowerPoint designer or delivering a compelling presentation that compels people to action. The latter is more lucrative. Therefore, once you have the bones of your slide show together, it can make sense to outsource slide building to someone who can do a better job in a fraction of the time you'd spend.

Presenting like a pro

Here's something that happens often with professionals and amateurs alike when using PowerPoint. You may have set up your equipment in a way that you find yourself walking between the beam cast by the data projector and the screen. As you walk, you create a temporary shadow on the screen. Your moving shadow naturally distracts people's attention and detracts from your presentation. So be careful to briefly practice *with your equipment turned on* to make sure you haven't set up that problem.

It's critical to take extra time to set up the room properly in advance. At times, room setup can be impossible to change, particularly if you know that the room will be packed with people. If your data projector is mounted on a center-front table with one screen center-front, wherever you stand, you may be obscuring someone's view. Be aware of this so you can change position from time to time and not penalize the same unfortunate viewers throughout your entire talk.

On occasion I've been able to set up the screen on one side of the stage—either left front or right front. A better scenario would be having two data projectors aimed at each side. This way, you have the stage to yourself and need not concern yourself with avoiding the light beam. If you have a choice between setting up a screen stage left or stage right, it's better to be on your left. This allows you to stand on the stage to your right. However, much depends on the room configuration; don't do this if circumstances don't support it.

By using slides only when you need them, you free yourself to move about the stage as you see fit. You can do this by positioning black (blank) slides where you don't want any visuals.

> To create black slides, insert a new slide. Select Normal View, click on Format, then Background, change the color to black, and then save.

I also recommend purchasing a remote mouse that can blank out a slide when you need to. It's very valuable. Using the "B" key noted earlier can be an alternative to this feature. In both cases, pressing "Forward" takes you back to where you were, as will any key on the keyboard.

Pitfalls when creating your slide show

Unfortunately, modern technology and common sense don't always go hand in hand; users often fall into one or more traps. Try to avoid the following common pitfalls:

1. Adding too many special effects; they detract from the central points you want to make.

2. Having a rigid format and inability to adjust (usually shorten) a presentation if necessary. You should be able to remove a few slides at short notice if your time gets cut. This means you have to plan ahead which slides can be eliminated. When you do, don't save your changes or you may lose those slides altogether. If you do save them, create a version A or version ___ (the name of your client, perhaps?)

3. Striding around while visuals are still on screen. When the visual is up, you want your audience to look at the slide, not you. Movement will cause them to look at you instead. When you decide it's time for them to look at you, remove the slide or black it out, and then move about.

4. Using an uncommon font. If you need to use someone else's machine at short notice, a standard font like Arial or Tahoma will ensure that the information on your slides is easily readable.

5. Not giving yourself enough time to set up. It creates unnecessary pressure for you.

6. Forgetting your backup CD or removable flash drive.

7. Selecting music that may irritate some members of your audience. Choosing the right music is a blend of knowing your audience, their age ranges, and the kind of audience message you want to get across.

8. Shaking your laser pointer. (Bear in mind that it's practically impossible to keep your hand completely still. Try it and you'll see what I mean!)

You're wise to have a Plan B in case technology lets you down. For example, what do you do if there is a power outage? Prepare yourself for the possibility of doing your entire presentation without slides. The other option is to cancel the presentation altogether. But that could have disastrous consequences for your reputation.

The principal secret is this: Don't use too many slides. That way you can move about freely most of the time. Remember, you're only using slides to illustrate and emphasize key points, not to replace you. Less is more. I'm not kidding.

Pitfalls when setting up your slide show

Technology exists to serve you, not the other way round. That means you don't want to spend your preparation time or your presentation time sorting out technology problems. So when setting up, make sure you reduce the possibility of these pitfalls happening:

- Not having an extension cord or plug points on hand, wasting valuable set-up time.
- Failing to test the equipment upon arrival yourself; relying on others.
- Forgetting to plug your laptop in to the power supply.
- Not noticing the projector is out of focus or crooked.
- Forgetting to cue your CDs, DVDs, or videos.
- Having problems with sound; get that sorted out well in advance.

Use of a mouse

When selecting a remote control or mouse to use, you have various options, including the cordless mouse and the remote mouse that doesn't have to be pointed directly at the computer. Choose a mouse that enables you to move freely without being hampered. A remote mouse is usually best for presentations and most have a laser pointer built in.

It is best to point the mouse in the direction of your receiver when changing slides, but try not to make it too obvious by, for instance, stretching your arm out each time you change a slide.

Make sure you carefully study the operation of your mouse. Imagine struggling to get it to work, only to find out that you've:

- Forgotten to switch it on
- Forgotten to attach the receiver
- Forgotten to insert batteries, or
- Left it on (or left the batteries in) after your last presentation, resulting in batteries going dead!

When you pack up your equipment, your mouse will likely get pressed against something in your bag, so taking out at least one of its batteries is a good idea. Just remember where you put it!

Which side to stand on?

It is accepted practice to face the audience and position your laptop to the left of you. The configuration of the stage does not always make this possible, so don't lose sleep over it if you have to break this rule. You do, however, want to position your laptop monitor where you can see it easily so if you need a cue, you don't find yourself turning toward the screen. On occasion, this will be impossible, too. Work within the limitations of your stage setup.

Marilyn Snyder is well known in the speaking profession as "The PowerPoint Lady." Here are some valuable tips from Marilyn:

Best advice: The most powerful advice I offer to presenters regarding the use of slide shows is simply this: If you can't use them well, don't use them at all. Why? Because poorly constructed slides detract from the positive image you want to portray.

Creating the right image: Audiences tend to judge the quality of both the speeches and the speakers by the quality of their slide shows and how well they present using their shows. If you're a good speaker with a bad set of slides, unfortunately you are rated poorly. If you're a good speaker with a good set of slides but you fumble with the equipment, make them dizzy with the laser pointer, and annoy the audience by not knowing your show or walking in front of the projector, you're still rated poorly. You can only win by delivering a great speech while expertly presenting a terrific visual PowerPoint show.

Worst mistake: What's the worst mistake you can make when giving a talk accompanied by a slide show? A presenter who reads from the screen invariably elicits the comment: "Instead of reading their slides to me, they could have handed out the printout for me to read back at the office and saved a lot of my time!" Think about it: You wouldn't hand out a copy of your speaker notes to the audience, would you? Then you mustn't put your speaker notes up on the screen. Instead, you need to move into the new century with your visuals, creating a different kind of show that consists of few words and many visuals.

Easy steps for great PowerPoint: Here's how to quickly improve the quality of your slide show in two steps: Start by eliminating all your speaker notes, the bullet points, and creating a few slides that have only a few words or a phrase on them. Then think about what your key points are and find a picture, chart, or other graphic that will help drive home your idea. For example, one of my PowerPoint design clients was talking about how adults need to be more like children, letting go of things that aren't important. To illustrate this idea, I found a picture of a child being swung joyfully by an adult. A second visual example is a client who was talking about office workers overwhelmed with paperwork. I located a picture of a woman sitting at a desk with papers stacked up to her ears, spilling off the desk, and piled behind her all the way to the ceiling. Point made—in far fewer than a thousand words!

—Marilyn Snyder, Interactive Presentations
www.IAPres.com

My perspective on slide shows

Long before slide shows existed in any form, people delivered effective presentations, which tells us two important things. First, the slide show only exists to *support* your message. Second, you can do without it. You may even plan how to do without it.

At the beginning of Chapter 4, I described a successful sales presentation that was conducted with no slide show at all. Remember, slide shows can be wonderful tools if used properly, but they also can be a serious impediment to your objective if used badly.

KEY LESSONS FROM CHAPTER 7

1. If used skillfully and set up properly, a PowerPoint slide show can do wonders for your overall presentation.

2. Setting up a slide show properly is time consuming. Do not allow preparing your slide show to dominate your preparation time to the extent that you forfeit practice time.

3. Setting up your room well in advance is highly recommended if you have the opportunity. Understand, though, that often circumstances prevent you from being able to accomplish this.

4. Don't walk across the beam of your data projector. If you do, you may as well put a sticker across your forehead that says, "I am an amateur!"

5. Buy your own remote mouse and use it for all your PowerPoint-driven presentations.

6. The onus is on you to check equipment *yourself* before going live. It's your show and your message. Control it!

7. Do not make your slides too wordy—short phrases and powerful images communicate best.

8. Although it is preferable to use your own laptop to drive your PowerPoint slide show, always have your show backed up on a flash drive and keep it

separate from your laptop—just in case! Also, using a standard font for the text on your slides will ensure your show can be used on most other computers.

9. Taking a course in PowerPoint is recommended if you intend using it often. If you first learn the basics before going for training, your learning will progress faster.

CHAPTER 8
THE POWER OF YOUR VOICE

"We are not won by arguments that we can analyze but by tone and
temper, by the manner which is the man himself."

—Poet Samuel Butler

Ignore your voice at your peril

The quality of your vocal presentation can make the difference
between success and failure. When preparing and practicing, you
usually center your focus on content. For those who know quite a
bit about this speaking business, your body language requires focus,
too. But how often is voice tone completely ignored? This can be a
serious oversight that proves costly for your career as a presenter.

Realize that the tone of your voice is one of your most convincing tools. It's your tone of voice that gives away your true feelings and triggers trust or suspicion in the listener. Listeners easily
pick up your authenticity (or lack of it) in your voice. Often, what's

mistaken for intuition is really the ears picking up on a tone that doesn't sound genuine. That's when warning bells go off.

Tone of voice is often referred to as "the characteristics of the voice." I believe these are the eight most important characteristics of any presenter's voice:

- Strong volume without shouting (voice projection)
- Moderate pace
- Warmth and empathy (related to pitch)
- Sincere expression
- Good use of inflection
- Words or phrases emphasized appropriately
- Clarity of speech (articulation)
- Appropriate pausing

If you can use each of these eight skills simultaneously, your voice becomes one of your best assets and will give your presentations the vocal edge they need to be successful.

There is, of course, no substitute for genuine enthusiasm and a smile!

Voice pitfalls

A common pitfall of presenters is to speak too fast, giving the audience little time to reflect on each idea. A more controlled pace helps them use their voices better, creates more inflection and emphasis, and gets the point across with more impact.

Ideally, you want to recreate your natural voice during a presentation—the one you automatically use when speaking with friends. The tension created by having to speak publicly often manifests in the vocal muscles tensing up, resulting in sounding unnatural—definitely a pitfall to avoid.

When rehearsing a talk or presentation, or simply wanting to hear how your voice sounds, record yourself and listen to the playback. It's best to use a camcorder or a digital voice recorder (DVC). The camcorder has the advantage of allowing you to view your body language as well. Because a DVC is compact, you can use it at short notice in places where it's difficult to set up a camcorder.

Some pitfalls to watch out for:

- Shouting—or coming across too softly

- Preaching—or coming across as aggressive or prescriptive

- Using a high, screechy, irritating voice—indicating you're tensing up

- Mumbling—resulting in your listeners straining to hear you

- Speaking too fast—risking the loss of your audience's attention

- Speaking too slowly—putting audience members to sleep

- Being monotonous—boring. You need more inflection in your voice and perhaps a variety of pace and volume.

- Failing to pause as appropriate—coming across as if you're in a hurry

The value of pausing

Master the art of pausing effectively. Taking a pause allows your listeners a moment to think about what you've just said. Because our brains think many times faster than we speak, we can do a great deal of thinking in just a few seconds.

Perhaps the most useful pause of all is the reflective pause at the end of an important sentence or statement. It causes listeners to think about what you have just said once before moving on to the next point. If you build in a reflective pause after making a point, listeners are more likely to internalize your key ideas and are less likely to miss the start of the next sentence. This also gives you a chance to gather your thoughts. Another kind of pause indicates that you may be selecting the right word or way to say something.

Professor Ronald Arden, a respected professional speaker coach and co-author of *The Power of Charm*, refers to several kinds of pauses this way:

1. The dramatic pause before an important revelation creates anticipation.

2. The reflective pause immediately after the dramatic statement gives the audience time to think about what you've just said.

3. One may pause before and/or after a word or phrase to highlight it.

4. Pausing for effect can be used to create humor or make you appear uncertain—on purpose, which creates a sense of spontaneity!

5. The sensory pause allows the audience to savor something delicious that you've just said.

6. You should also pause in order to relinquish control, for instance after asking, "Are there any questions?"

Pausing is sometimes used to allow people to quiet down before you proceed or before an announcement. Create tension or expectation before beginning by using the "pause for effect."

Care of the voice

Your voice is a delicate precision instrument. If you present regularly, taking the best possible care of it is absolutely non-negotiable. Avoid at all cost getting involved in cheerleader-type activities that cause you to shout or scream until you're hoarse. This can temporarily damage your throat, larynx, and vocal chords, becoming permanent if you do this kind of activity frequently.

Voice capabilities

If you consider the extraordinary capabilities of the human voice, you will be astounded at its versatility. There is no other sound instrument, musical or other, that has ever been created with more than a fraction of the capability of the voice. This may explain why the best singers in the world get paid many times more than the best pianists or violinists. Similarly, a performance by a comedian almost always involves tremendous vocal agility. As a presenter, you owe it to yourself to look after this fine instrument and teach it to do what you require of it. With a bit of coaxing and proper warm-up and practice techniques, you'll have a finely tuned instrument.

Warming up

Actors are taught to warm up as part of their drama education; opera singers won't perform if they have to take the stage without an adequate voice warm-up. The principle is similar to distance runners starting a long run. They pace themselves slowly on the first few miles to warm up the muscles, gradually building their speed. Because speakers don't have the luxury of starting slowly, the voice warm-up serves as the needed "slow start."

Warm up properly using the following breathing, voice toning, and articulation exercises.

Breathing exercises: It's of utmost importance that you have your breathing under control, both as a means of remaining relaxed and projecting your voice correctly. It's especially important that you breathe from your diaphragm, as shallow breath (from the chest only) both creates tension and raises the pitch of your voice.

Practice these three breathing exercises regularly and especially before giving a presentation:

1. Place your hand on your diaphragm and hiss: *sss, ffff, sss, fff* over and over again, starting slowly and then speeding up. The idea is to feel your diaphragm moving in as you say the *sss,* relaxing for a moment and going in on the next *fff,* and taking small breaths in between. This exercises your diaphragm and makes you conscious of using it when you breathe.

2. Breathe in slowly through the nose for a slow count of four, hold for four counts, exhale (through the mouth) over four counts, hold for four, and gradually increase the count to up to eight. Again, place your hand on your diaphragm to make sure the breath is coming from there and

not only from your chest. Feel your diaphragm pushing out as you breathe in and vice versa.

3. Controlling the "out breath" is vital when speaking publicly. Your aim is to have just the right amount of breath for each sentence. You certainly don't want to appear breathless or have to gasp for air mid-sentence! A good way to practice breath control is to count "1." "1, 2." "1, 2, 3." and so on, going as high as you like and then down to "1" again. Counting up to 30 is good and up to 50 is even better to increase your air capacity (but it will take some time). Take in only as much breath as you need for each count. Don't leave any air in your lungs after each count.

For the best results, do exercises 2 and especially 3 lying on your back. When you speak publicly, be aware of creating volume and warmth by breathing from your diaphragm, rather than speaking from your head. Allow your chest to resonate as you breathe deeply.

Voice toning: If you have a warm, deep voice, you have an advantage over speakers whose voices are high and squeaky, which can be irritating to listeners. But if your voice is high-pitched, don't despair. With effort, you can develop a rich, warm voice. Either way, warm up your vocals with these four exercises.

1. This exercise is excellent for deepening your pitch. Lie on your back and hum mmmmmm on one note, softly at first and at your lowest pitch, pushing the air gently out using your diaphragm. Consciously open your throat. Your lips

should vibrate. Be aware of a vibration in your chest. Then do the same on higher and higher notes. Increase your volume slowly. The lower pitches might sound funny at first if you push your voice pitch down, but keep going. The resonance will improve the more you practice. Be sure to do this gently so you don't strain your voice.

2. Do the same exercise with each of the sounds *aah*, *eee*, *oooh*, and *oh*, making sure your throat is open. Feel the epiglottis at the back of your throat lifting up. If your throat tightens, you could strain your voice. Again, aim for a sound that resonates in your chest, especially on the lower notes. Note how the sound goes more into your head the higher you go.

3. Hum some scales, starting on your lowest note, then your second lowest note, and so on, using first the mmmm-mmm sound and then the vowel sounds, always keeping your throat open and breathing from your diaphragm.

4. When you get to actually presenting, be aware of "placing" the sound in your chest rather than in your head and projecting from there—but not rigidly, of course, for you don't want to speak in a monotone. Practice this by speaking a few sentences fairly loudly, feeling the resonance in your head on the higher notes and in your chest on the lower ones, accompanied by a vibration in the area in which you "place" the sound. If you keep up these exercises, your resonance will improve and even the high notes will resonate with warm undertones.

5. Oh, and if you have a nasal twang, this technique will help you to overcome that as well.

Articulation: If you mumble, audience members are likely to miss much of what you say. The trick is to get your tongue and lips agile. Do these nine exercises (when no one is looking):

1. Open your mouth wide—into an artificial grin—consciously stretching your lips, then purse them, stretch them again, and so on. Do this several times.

2. Stretch in another direction by opening your mouth as wide as you can, making an O.

3. Close your mouth and blow up your cheeks. Hold for a few seconds.

4. Make a *prrrr* sound like a horse, feeling your lips vibrate.

5. Stick out your tongue and move it quickly from side to side, keeping it straight.

6. Then curl it sidewise, flipping it over in your mouth, first one way, and then the other. The faster you can go, the more agile your tongue will be.

7. With your mouth open at first, move your tongue in a circle 10 times around the inside of your cheeks and lips (in front of the teeth). Then go in the opposite direction. Then do the same with your mouth closed. You'll be surprised how quickly your tongue gets tired!

8. Stick out your tongue and try to move only the tip.

9. Warmed up? Now sing some more scales, one consonant at a time: For example: (ascending) *pih pih pih pih . . . peh peh peh peh . . . pah pah pah pah . . . puh puh puh puh . . .* (and descending) *pih pih pih pih . . . peh peh peh peh . . . pah pah pah pah . . . puh puh puh puh . . . paah.* Do the same with B, K and G, T and D, F and V, S and Z, L, M and N, and even NG (with your epiglottis!). You will soon feel which parts of your mouth need exercise most.

Do all of these exercises regularly—as often as time will allow—first to develop resonance and vocal ability, and then to maintain these qualities. Don't despair if you don't get immediate results. It takes time to hone one's voice, just as it takes time to learn a musical instrument. And, of course, do them just before doing a presentation—but for heaven's sake not as you're walking on stage, unless you want to give your audience cause for a great deal of mirth. It's best to do the main warm-up at home or in your hotel room before going to your presentation venue. Then do a five-minute refresher just before walking on stage.

Replacing liquids

Speakers may blow out the equivalent of about a seven-ounce glass of water every half hour, so it makes sense to regularly replace the liquid you're losing. Have a glass of warm to room-temperature water beside you at all times. Most often, venue staff members bring you a glass of water half-filled with ice cubes. Thank them kindly, then with a charming smile politely ask them to bring you a glass of unchilled water with no ice. Some venues provide bottled water. If so, make sure yours hasn't been chilled. If possible, avoid teas and coffees before you speak, and under no circumstances go near a drop of alcohol. All of these dehydrate your body.

If you've eaten a meal before your presentation or during a break, drinking a cup of hot water will help clear your trachea and open up your vocal cords. Sip this from time to time to keep your voice warm and lubricated.

Microphones

My rule of thumb is that voice amplification is desirable for audiences of 40 or more people, or where the room can comfortably seat 60 people or more cinema style. This rule can be adjusted according to the size and shape of the room as well as the duration of your presentation. For example, if you have a relatively small room with adequate acoustics packed with 55 people cinema-style for under an hour, you can get away with no amplification. Also factor the length of your presentation. The longer it is, the more strain your voice will take.

Using a microphones however, can be disastrous for the uneducated. A hand-held mic with a cable may give you a clear sound, but unless you stand still for your entire presentation, the cable may create problems for you, making you feel (and look) like a lion tamer at a circus. You also need to hold the microphone slightly away from your mouth and avoid blowing in to it, as this creates "popping" sounds.

All forms of wireless microphones have frequency issues you need to understand if you supply your own microphone, but wireless is certainly the way to go. The lapel microphone remains popular, but it is restrictive as the volume recedes slightly when your head is turned to one side or the other. If you haven't comfortably attached your receiver to your clothing, it may crackle during your talk.

I find a high quality headset microphone works best. My favorite is the Shure-compatible Countryman headset. It is so light and thin that, after a short while, neither you nor your audience realizes it's there! But its greatest advantage is that the mouthpiece stays with you when you move your head, resulting in no variation in your volume. I regard my Countryman to be one of the best investments I've ever made. I take it with me to all engagements involving 40 or more participants. I know my equipment works, it's easy to wear, and helps me avoid headaches that come with using a strange mic.

Remember that the transmitter (to which your microphone is connected and that hooks onto a belt or goes in to a jacket pocket) uses a lot of battery power. A long-life penlight battery set will give you a maximum of four hours, so replace it with fresh batteries before each presentation. You can also buy good quality rechargeable batteries with the charger. These save in battery costs and the inconvenience of having to constantly purchase batteries.

Another valuable but inexpensive tool is a battery tester, which is especially useful if you can't remember how long you've used a set of batteries. It's best to always carry a set of four fully charged batteries with you.

Amplifiers

An easy way to kill a good presentation is to project your voice through a poor quality amplifier. You don't want your voice to sound "tinny" or to "boom." By purchasing your own professional quality amplifier and having it on standby for local engagements (which I call "home games"), you allow yourself an additional option that could prove vitally important. When you're "playing away," venue or event organizers should provide amplifiers of professional quality. Even though they usually provide microphones too, I take mine with me and simply hook it up to their systems. If you can ascertain that the sound technician at the venue has a receiver that's compatible with your transmitter, you can safely avoid lugging the extra weight with you. Especially, when you speak "at home," bring your own receiver as a back up, whether or not you are supplying the amplifier.

When setting up your speakers, ensure they're positioned in front of you and facing the audience so you don't encounter feedback when you turn to the side. Again, if it is a large venue and your speaker cables aren't long enough for you to position the far-side speaker in front, you may find yourself dealing with feedback through your talk—an awkward and distracting problem. I suggest planning up front, and consider carrying at least one extended-length speaker cable with your amplifier.

Marija Ruygrok, one of South Africa's foremost voice coaches, offers this advice:

Your voice is the means by which you express yourself, tell your stories, and persuade. It is a powerful tool that few people think to improve or master. I like to think of my voice as a musical instrument that I need to learn to "play" well. Anyone can make a noise on a violin or piano, but it takes exercise and practice to really master these instruments and play a piece of music that will inspire and uplift an audience.

When we present, audience members are listening to how we speak and are asking themselves, "Does this person sound credible? Does he or she sound confident, enthusiastic, committed?" We might have the most profound content supported by sound data and relevant examples, but if we fail to deliver the information well—by speaking too softly, mumbling, rushing through the content, and boring our audiences with monotony—then all that potential greatness will be lost.

A brief comment on accents—your accent is part of your personality, background, and culture. I would never recommend that one "gets rid of" an accent. It adds color and uniqueness to speech. Rather, one should work on improving clarity by clear articulation. If you have a strong accent or are speaking to foreign audiences who might find your accent strange, speak even slower than normal at the beginning of your presentation. This will give the audience time to tune in to your particular accent.

It's never too late to work on your voice and improve your speech. Find a good voice coach who can identify your vocal strengths and weaknesses. You will be amazed at the improvement that a few focused sessions can make so you "speak the speech," as Hamlet entreats the actors, ". . . trippingly on the tongue."

—Marija Ruygrok, Director of Accents
www.accents.co.za

KEY LESSONS FROM CHAPTER 8

1. Tone of voice and voice characteristics indicate the true meaning behind the words. Listeners detect a myriad of emotions from the voice.

2. Two of the most important components are pace and volume. You want to develop a moderate, medium-pace delivery, and project well without shouting.

3. Using the pause is a vital part of vocal delivery. The best presenters use pauses skillfully by knowing where and why to use them.

4. Your voice is a precision instrument that should be treated with care and respect.

5. If you warm up your voice before going on stage, it performs better and for longer. Use the exercises provided in this chapter to warm it up before each practice and presentation, and to assist you in areas you want to improve.

6. If a microphone is available, use it, but make sure that it works and that the settings suit your voice. It is seldom necessary to shout when you have a microphone. Investing in your own microphone is a "must" if you present regularly.

7. Ensure that you have a glass of water—preferably room temperature or warm and never with ice—with you on stage!

8. The quality of your equipment needs to be good, as a poor voice reproduction will badly affect your presentation.

CHAPTER 9

CONNECTING WITH YOUR AUDIENCE

"One of the best ways to connect with someone's mind is through their feelings."

— Professor Ronald Arden, professional speaker and coach

Establishing rapport

The value of quickly establishing rapport with your audience cannot be overestimated. It's fundamental to the success of any presentation. It not only relaxes you, the speaker, but also gets the audience aligned with the objectives and flow of your talk.

A popular method is using "ice breakers" in the form of asking questions and getting audience responses. Another is to get audience members to participate in games at the beginning. Telling a humorous joke, if properly planned and used cleverly, can be effective but it can also backfire if it's not told convincingly and lacks purpose (see Using humor well).

Whichever you choose, involving your audience as participants gets them to make a kind of commitment up front. Remember, your chances of persuading people to do what you suggest are determined far more by whether they like and trust you than by what you say. This is often decided by how you open. So get involved with audience members from the start and talk *to* them, not *at* them. The degree of your success will be determined by how well you connect with them.

The power of a strong start

When first presenting yourself, one technique is to simply stand in front of the audience for a few seconds. Establish a "me and you" feel. Then make a strong opening (or headline) statement. For instance, what if *The Power of Positive Thinking* guru Dr. Norman Vincent Peale started his talk in 1952 (a mere seven years after World War II ended) by saying this: "Imagine a Europe in 50 years' time with one single currency and virtually no borders?" Would that grab their attention right from the start?

It's widely taught that it takes seven seconds to make a first impression and that initial impression lasts forever. What you wear is a big part of this; so is how you walk on to the stage and start your talk. Make sure you catch your audience's attention with an opening statement that's clear, provocative, and delivered with confidence. If appropriate, and it often is, adding a smile can add weight to the impact of your introduction.

When you succeed in engaging your audience from the start, it's easier to keep them with you for the duration. Beyond the first-impression stage, the content—and how you deliver it—takes over.

A while back, I made a substantial investment in my speaking career. I paid for one-on-one coaching with Ronald Arden, a man considered "the best" by many of the world's most highly paid speakers. What astounded me was seeing where his focus lay.

"Show me how you start off," commanded Professor Arden. And so I did, over and over again, until I delivered it the way he wanted. When we were finished, he felt pleased and proclaimed, "A morning well spent, methinks!"

Six months later, I addressed the meeting of the Irish chapter of the Professional Speaker's Association of Great Britain at the Guinness Storehouse in Dublin. Right after, I received this feedback from its president, Brian Matthews: "Paul, you started so powerfully that it didn't matter much what you said after that!"

Well, I guess his comment could be taken one of two ways. I took it as a compliment, but I've been paying extra attention to the impact of the rest of my talk since then!

> "Laugh at yourself and at life. Not in the spirit of derision or whining self-pity, but as a remedy, a miracle drug, that will ease your pain, cure your depression, and help you to put in perspective that seemingly terrible defeat and worry with laughter at your predicaments, thus freeing your mind to think clearly toward the solution that is certain to come."
>
> —Sales guru Og Mandino, author of
> *The Greatest Salesman in the World*

Using humor well

You'll have a distinct advantage over other speakers if you use humor well and appropriately. By that, I mean that telling a joke for the sake of getting a laugh is inappropriate. To be appropriate, it must fit into your content and helps to make a point.

By contrast, humor that doesn't work puts you in an awkward place striving to recover. Only you will know how confident you are about using humor successfully. If you know that you use humor well socially, you should have no trouble pulling off a funny story or a one-liner to round off your presentation. My most hallowed principle is to practice your quip on a "safe" audience (family and friends) before using it during a presentation. If it bombs, it doesn't mean it will never work; it just may need restructuring. If after several trials, it still doesn't work, try something else. No use getting attached to a dud!

But even rules are not cast in concrete. During my Dublin presentation titled "Using humor in your presentations," I thought up a humorous story during my flight over and told it for the first time during my talk. I didn't expect much of a laugh; it was intended to illustrate that one should test one's jokes on a safe audience first. My story goes as follows:

Two chaps, one of them an Irishman named Paddy, are having a beer in a London pub.

The other one says: "So, how is business in Dublin, Paddy?

To which Paddy replies: "Terrible, terrible!"

"But what's the matter, Paddy? Everyone knows the Irish economy is booming . . ."

"I know, I know," replies Paddy. "That's what's so frustrating."

"Well, what are you trying to sell them then?"

"Sunglasses!" he replies.

I expected some muffled laughter, no more than that. For those unfamiliar with Ireland, the joke is that the sun doesn't get a "look in" that often so selling sunglasses in a place where there's not much sun borders on crass stupidity. This Irish audience understood the implications of Paddy's business decision all too well.

On this occasion, my Irish audience literally roared with laughter. That surprised me, as I had never tested this joke, but it did give me quite a kick. Truth is, I got lucky on this one. I knew it was untested and could have gone down like a lead balloon.

Sometimes, in the right context, perhaps with appropriate regional references, your story or quip will hit the mark. Remember, if you don't get a huge laugh, it doesn't necessarily mean it wasn't appreciated. Some people are simply more effusive than others. If your story makes a good point and ties in with your theme, use it—especially if it's original.

I understand that some speakers feel uncomfortable using humor. If this is you, don't feel obliged to plan it into your talk. If you're relaxed during your presentation, humor will likely arrive by chance!

As a rule, I suggest avoiding certain categories of humor—namely discriminatory stories, stale (old) or dirty jokes, and anything involving swearing. Also avoid making jokes at an audience member's expense. I find, however, that audiences usually appreciate a self-deprecating story.

Be aware of several categories of humor and work to develop your own brand. If you like telling "set piece" jokes, for example, the audience's response will have a lot to do with your timing. Here, "set piece" refers to something that's been well rehearsed rather than a spontaneous attempt at humor. I liken it to the skill of soccer set-piece specialist David Beckham, who became famous for his ability to score from "set piece" free kicks, which often changed the course of a game. As Beckham got older, he seemed to get better at scoring from these free kicks. Similarly, the more times you tell a specific joke or funny story, the better you get. To me, this illustrates the point that if you tell a "set piece" story within context and do it well, it can have a powerful impact.

Light-heartedness is a useful alternative to jokes or one-liners. You may have an amusing slant on a topic that works well in a particular context. For example, I recently observed a presentation skills student delivering a two-minute impromptu speech on his hobbies. Trouble was he didn't have a hobby, so he used the 60 seconds to explain why he didn't have one, the next 40 seconds explaining how he typically invested his time, and then concluded, to howls of laughter, that since he mowed his lawn every weekend, his hobby must be gardening!

Many presenters find that when they're in tune with their audiences, spontaneous humor comes naturally. The spontaneity enhances your delivery and the audience's appreciation of your style. During a light-hearted moment, some of the funniest responses come from audience members themselves. I acknowledge these outbursts positively because it enhances the overall mood.

During one presentation, I confided how I'd so focused on the content of my talk that I absentmindedly put on my jacket before I put on my shirt. Realizing my error, I removed my jacket and then put on the wrong shirt. An audience member spontaneously chirped, "Your shirt looks fine!" Laughter followed. I retorted, "Thanks, but this is not the shirt—I changed into the right one!" More laughter—and I knew they were with me.

Starting with humor can be great, but be sure to use a well-tested story that's guaranteed to get a laugh—and make sure you get it right.

Feedback and evaluations

Some years ago, I was delivering a talk in a small South African town called Empangeni in Kwazulu-Natal. The thickset man sitting directly in my line of vision spent practically the entire presentation with his chin resting in his left hand, propped up by his elbow on the table in front of him. He appeared totally bored. I managed to get only one half-smile out of him two-thirds of my way through the talk.

At the end of my presentation, he stood up and, to my surprise, addressed the audience and me for about 90 seconds. He thanked me for coming to Empangeni and affirmed the tremendous value he'd derived from the talk—stating he was certain everyone else valued it, too. I was taken aback, but I'd learned this valuable lesson: from reading obvious reactions—body language, facial expressions, and vocal responses—you never know whom you've impacted and how.

Not all audiences are the same. I have often seen a good performance receiving a high evaluation and the same performance, presented even better at a different location with a different audience, receiving a much lower evaluation. Depending on the context of your presentation, evaluations can be extremely valuable sources of feedback, but should always be taken in good humor. As presenters we tend to focus an inordinate amount of attention on the two negative evaluations instead of the 30 or 90 good ones. An insightful comment is of more value than a 10-out-of-10 score—and you should be gracious enough to bask in the positive testimonials as well as learning from the criticism.

Making eye contact

When you conduct a one-on-one meeting of any kind, you'll normally start by shaking hands and establishing eye contact. The traditional handshake has its origins in the distant past—it indicates you are unarmed and come in peace. But it's the eye contact that establishes rapport. By maintaining frequent eye contact, you increase trust, thus creating a climate for business. People in western culture instinctively distrust people who avoid eye contact, especially when first greeting them.

As a presenter, your eye contact options are affected by the room layout and audience size, so take everything into consideration before you start your talk.

It's natural to favor the people in the middle with more eye contact than the rest of your audience. If there are several rows, it's easy to accidentally ignore people at the front. Because it's impossible to make personal eye contact with every member of a large audience, make sure you look at different sections of attendees frequently and don't ignore any one. Sometimes critical decision makers sit to one side. It is a good idea to establish in advance who they are so you can make sufficient eye contact with them.

If you use cue cards, practice glancing at your card briefly as you end a sentence to get your next cue, written in the form of a trigger word or two. Pause to breathe, look up, and then continue, making seamless eye contact all the while.

Always remember to speak *to* the audience, not *at* them. Eye contact is without question your most powerful rapport-creation tool. It keeps people engaged, which is exactly how you want them to be throughout your presentation.

Basic audience requirements

While you have made a substantial investment in time and money to put together and deliver your presentation, remember that your audience is also investing time and money to listen to you. You can best repay them by being conscious of their requirements.

They expect a well-structured, interesting presentation with humor and perhaps good visuals or multimedia. They also appreciate your sticking to your allotted time. If something relatively innocuous goes wrong, it can become the focus of the experience for some audience members. So getting the basic audience requirements right will avoid disruptions to your presentation.

Also prepare what to do if logistical problems occur. While giving a keynote speech to fellow speakers, I experienced a power cut seven minutes into my talk, seconds after I'd shown them a video clip. I continued as if nothing had happened. Two minutes later, the generator kicked in and I simply went back to using my PowerPoint. The feedback showed that they, as fellow speakers, had learned a lot about how to handle power outages from what I did.

Be sure the air conditioner is set to the right temperature in advance (71° to 73°F is usually best). Ensure the seating is comfortable and that chairs aren't squashed too close together. Test to see if people can see both you and the screen clearly and change it if doing so is within your control.

Ask your introducer to politely remind the audience to switch off cell phones, tell them the location of restrooms and coffee stations, and note where meals will be served as well as the agenda. If the host venue supplies parking vouchers, it should be mentioned here.

By handling logistics efficiently, you show your audience that you care. This not only helps establish rapport; it also puts people's minds at rest and allows them to focus on what you have to say. That's a good way to start persuading them to your way of thinking!

Marie Farrugia, a professional speaker from Melbourne, Australia, who specializes in life balance, shares her approach to connecting with her audiences:

In March 2002, as a fledgling speaker, I attended my first National Speaker's Association of Australia convention. One keynote speaker, Max Dixon, urged us to "be the best YOU that you can be" when delivering to an audience.

I had always been able to pick those speakers who seemed more "genuine" and in rapport with the audience, but I was unable to pinpoint the magic ingredient that made them so.

During my initial years of presenting, I was very self-conscious during my delivery and kept in mind my stagecraft, what I said, how I said it, where I was up to, and what came next. In other words, I was totally in my head the whole time because I believed that would make for a polished delivery. After a while, I realized that in order to fully connect with my audience, I had to disengage from my head and give from my heart.

How can you do this? Simple. Know your content and rehearse your stories so that when you step on to the stage, you can "go with the flow" and give the audience the best YOU that you can be . . . totally from the heart.

Not only does this work for the audience, but also for me—because I am being genuine and believable and enjoying the experience!

—Marie Farrugia, NSAA Victoria Speaker of the Year 2006

www.timeforyou.com.au

Audience needs—why they come

When we present, our focus is all too often on ourselves. It shouldn't be. If we start with the needs of our audience, we invariably give them value and sufficient information to help them make the decisions we guide them to make.

Even weeks before you start your preparation, ask, "Why will people come to listen to me? What do they want from my presentation?" When you have answered these questions, you will have discovered exactly what you need to do.

If you use industry jargon, consider whether people in the audience might not understand this jargon. For instance, the terms bytes, RAM, and hard drive are familiar to Information Technology people and computer users, but beginners might think they've come to a presentation on sheep farming by mistake!

Be prepared for the possibility of hostile audiences or individuals and don't allow yourself to get involved in an argument with a member of your audience. It you do, it undermines everything you say thereafter. Rather, acknowledge the person's point of view and move on without allowing their interjections to become an issue. (Look for techniques and advice in Chapter 10.)

Connecting with audience members is fundamental to your presentation's success. Remember, it shouldn't be about you or how you deliver; it's about them and what they do after hearing your message. Make a strong connection and create rapport. It's your first job on stage.

Exceptions to the rules

Chapter 6 emphasized the importance of the correct attire and effective body language. These are best practice rules that should be followed. So should the suggestion about dressing one step up from the audience.

But a minority of speakers use a technique that deliberately breaks the rules. One example is South African scenario planning speaker Clem Sunter. He often takes the stage looking scruffy and puts his hands in his pockets while delivering his talk. However, his content is excellent, his talks well structured; he speaks well and uses great stories. He is light hearted and connects with his audience in an authentic way. And he shows respect for his meeting planner and audience by finishing within his allotted time frame—a true professional. Clem's ultra casual approach has become his brand and it works for him. He is a heavily booked speaker.

KEY LESSONS FROM CHAPTER 9

1. Establishing audience rapport early in your presentation will relax you and make your presentation more enjoyable and persuasive.

2. A powerful start is vital in getting your audience's attention immediately. A headline-like opening statement, even a controversial one, can achieve this.

3. Presenters often involve audience members in discussions or games to establish rapport.

4. Humor, if used appropriately, can get your audience into a jovial mood. People are receptive to new messages when they're engaged and laughing.

5. Evaluations are good indicators of your performance, but must be viewed as subjective feedback. Keep in mind that diverse audiences in various contexts evaluate a presentation quite differently than each other.

6. Eye contact is one of your most powerful tools of persuasion and engagement.

7. An audience that's physically comfortable and eager to get the information promised is a receptive audience. That's why focusing on your audience's needs is vital. Presenters who focus on their own needs don't understand this.

8. Ensure you clearly understand why most of your audience members have come to listen to you.

9. "Best practice" guidelines should generally be followed. When you've joined the celebrity ranks, you're welcome to experiment with them, but if you're delivering a business presentation, following "the rules" works best.

CHAPTER 10
TURNING QUESTION TIME TO YOUR ADVANTAGE

"I learnt long ago never to wrestle with a pig. You get dirty and, besides, the pig likes it."

—Irish playwright George Bernard Shaw

The presentation graveyard

If you've ever been asked a tricky question by a four year old and answered it less than adequately, you've probably received the response, "Why?" This meant you had to have another go at answering the same question. And if you blew your second chance, the child might have kept you going with "why?" all afternoon, until you eventually lost patience with your little tormentor. If you're a parent, you've probably experienced this more than once. Know what's interesting? The child is in control every time. You see, the one who asks the questions is always in control. So why would you even consider handing over control of your presentation to your audience by introducing a time for questions?

Well, here are a few good reasons you might want to.

Why allow questions at all?

Question time can be the death of a presentation. It can put the presenter on the defensive almost immediately—that is, unless you have a strategy for dealing with question time. The reason for including it must be to give you the opportunity to further support your presentation by giving the audience a chance to obtain specific information from you or raise concerns. A well-prepared presenter will skillfully use Q&A time to achieve the objectives of the presentation.

Questions from the audience can be valuable in helping the presenter re-engage the attendees and make it real for them. You don't want it to feel like a canned, scripted presentation.

Also, setting a question time means you can defer any questions to this allotted slot, so the structure of your talk won't get derailed by questions taken during the middle of it.

If someone raises a question during the presentation relating to subject matter you're still coming to, respond by saying, "Please hold on to that important question. I will be taking questions during the second half of the presentation" or "Good question: there is actually a better spot to deal with that a little later on, so let me respond to you more fully then."

You might also announce in your introduction that you expect people to have questions during the presentation. Ask them to please make a note of their questions and pose them during the allotted time.

Different types of questions are meant to:

- Clarify information on a certain point
- Raise an issue that has not been covered
- Suggest an alternative point of view

The manner in which people ask questions gives you a clue about the purpose of the question. For example, does the question seek information, raise concerns, test you, challenge your facts, or oppose your proposal?

Alan Stevens, The Media Coach, shares these valuable insights on approaching question time:

Handling questions at the end of a presentation is often the worst fear of new (and not so new) presenters. But, like everything else in life, planning is the key to success.

Before you give a presentation, write down the five worst possible questions you could get and how you would deal with them. Rehearse them with friends and colleagues. And remember that you don't have to answer absolutely everything—it's quite acceptable to say something like, "That requires a fairly complex response. If you can see me afterward, I'll be happy to talk it over with you."

Stay calm. Remember, there are no stupid questions. Always show your questioner respect (though it can be difficult, especially if you know he or she has a particular bias). Even worse, questioners might make remarks you find irritating. Keep calm and ignore any unpleasantness. Answer the question directly and factually, without being drawn into criticizing someone else's opinion.

Never use sarcasm or belittle a questioner. If you do, onlookers side with the questioner, not you. Focus on the words they've said, not on them as people. If you strongly disagree with their stance, say something like, "I understand your point of view, but I don't share it. Let me explain how I see things." Don't make any assumptions. Simply accept the questioner's presuppositions, correcting them gently if necessary.

Always smile and thank questioners for making their points. Even if you are seething with rage and indignation inside, don't show it. You will win far more respect if you maintain a professional image.

—Alan Stevens, FPSA, The Media Coach
www.mediacoach.co.uk

Handling questions

A well-prepared presenter anticipates audience concerns and areas of interest, and addresses them during the presentation. Anticipate questions you might not wish to cover up front and prepare your answers in advance so that you are not taken by surprise. For unanticipated questions, a direct answer is best.

If you're asked a question you struggle to answer, admit that you don't know, offer to find out the answer, and get back to them. Release yourself from the burden of having to know everything and seize the opportunity to demonstrate your honesty and sincerity. Under no circumstances should you "wing it" or guess the answer.

When the floor is opened for questions there is sometimes a pregnant pause until someone breaks the ice. You can use one of two techniques here:

1. Have a FAQ (frequently asked question) prepared in advance and pose it as the first question by saying, "I am often asked . . ." Then answer the question. This should take about 40 seconds, giving your audience time to formulate questions to follow your opening one.

2. Allow about 10 seconds to wait for a question; someone usually comes to the fore. If no one does, hold up a currency note (amount depending on how much you can afford!) and offer it to the first person who asks a relevant question.

Once the questions start flowing, you need a strategy for dealing with them that will ensure you remain in control of the session, even if you are faced with a hostile audience or encounter a few tough questions. One time-tested method for doing this is known by its acronym, TRACT.

Make TRACT your tool

When handling questions, it's vital to listen attentively to the question, then follow these guidelines:

Thank the questioner
Repeat the question
Answer the question
Confirm satisfaction
Thank the questioner again

Let's examine each step in the TRACT process:

Thank the questioner—It's polite, acknowledges the person's interest, and shows you're not afraid of the question. It tells the audience whom they are addressing and encourages more questions—everyone wants to see what will happen to the brave soul who goes first! But, most importantly, it puts you in control and on the front foot.

Repeat every question through the mic (if you are using one)—This is important. First, it confirms to the questioner that you've heard correctly. Secondly, it allows people on the other side of the room to hear the question. Thirdly, it allows you to summarize what may have been a long question. Fourthly, and most important, it gives you extra time to organize your thoughts and give a measured response.

Answer the question—Give a concise, credible, confident answer. By doing so you support your position and show the questioners who's in control—YOU! It's important that your answer actually answers the questions.

Confirm satisfaction—By checking that you've answered adequately, you confirm that the questioners are satisfied and you further assert your control. If they say "yes," go to the final step in the Q&A process. If they say "no," ask them to clarify their questions further and then fill in the missing parts of your answers. Then go on to the concluding "thank you."

Thank them again—This confirms that you're confident and in control. You're then able to turn to the area from which to take your next question without appearing rude.

In the event you're presenting with a microphone, it is courteous (logistics permitting) to provide a roving mic that's handed to each questioner. Alert a member of your team to move the roving mic between questioners. It won't do to have you rushing about like a headless chicken, rendering yourself breathless in the process!

Warning: During presentation skills training, your facilitator usually insists that you use TRACT at question time. This allows you to practice the skill and get used to using it appropriately. It doesn't mean you have to use TRACT in every situation—use your discretion for this. For a one-on-one presentation, TRACT is inappropriate. The general rule is that the larger or more hostile your audience, the more likely you are to need TRACT to stay in control.

When you learn to use this tool in a way that sounds natural, make TRACT a wonderful friend to have in your back pocket. So it sounds natural, sometimes swap the first "thank you" with "repeat," or thank them only when you're taking a second question from the same person. It's all too easy to forget that you have TRACT in your back pocket, so remind yourself before you go live.

Be careful of becoming so focused on the tool itself that you forget to listen actively to the question. You are most likely to make this mistake at the "answer" stage and find out about it at the "confirm satisfaction" stage when the response from an audience member shows you got it wrong.

Look intently at the questioners and nod your head in acknowledgment from time to time while they speak. This keeps you focused on them.

Staying in control

The length of your answer often defines, from an audience perspective, whether you are in control or not. People who are unsure of themselves often waffle on at length, subconsciously believing that the more information they impart, the more convincing they will be. Nothing can be further from reality. The most convincing answers are concise and "to the point." A 30-second answer is, in most instances, quite sufficient. Where a questioner asks you more than one question at a time, it is often easier to answer the last part first and work your way back. That way, if you forget the first part of the question, you can ask the person to repeat it for you.

Depending on the nature of the audience, question time can sometimes throw the presenter a few curve balls. A confident "thank you, I'm glad you asked that question!" will often disarm the smart Alec, but be sure you have an answer.

Another technique is to refer the question to an associate who may be an expert on the subject. Be careful of putting your associate on the spot, though. You might say, "John is in fact the expert on this aspect of the project. John, would you care to answer the lady's question, or would you prefer to chat with her afterward?"

Do not allow question time to get out of hand. Particularly, don't allow one individual to hijack your presentation. If it's clear this is happening, isolate the questioner by turning your body toward the other side of the room for the next question. Unless a specific time has been set aside for questions, up to five questions from the floor are usually sufficient, unless you have factored in more time. Any additional questions can be directed to you after the presentation.

Never end with "that's all we have time for, folks!" Your time frame is *your* problem, not theirs, and this may annoy those who still have their hands up. Rather, say something like this: "I'm going to move in to the conclusion now and ask that any further questions be directed to me in the lobby afterward." That way, no one is likely to be offended.

Finally, question time can be used as a time buffer. For example, if you have an hour to present, and you have factored in 20 minutes for question time and your segment starts 10 minutes late (I hope through no fault of yours!), you can shorten question time to 10 minutes. Then you won't have to rush your presentation.

Warren Evans, past president of the Global Speakers Federation (formerly the International Federation of Professional Speakers) and past president of the Canadian Association of Professional Speakers (CAPS), has this to share regarding Q&A time:

Having bravely, or foolishly, waded into this realm with audiences from all around the world over the years, I've had the good fortune to make just about every mistake in the book and thus learned from the ultimate master teacher: experience.

Here are a two key things I've learned:

1. Never end with Q&A (which is where most people, including agenda-setters, intuitively put it).
2. Always stop and say, "I'd be happy to take a few questions at this point before I get to my concluding remarks." Let them know that you will have more to say after they get their turn. In this way, you end your session the way you want to, without looking like you are scrambling to "recover" from something

that happened during Q&A. And you get the chance to put questions into perspective with the rest of what you've said. In your final five minutes you summarize the entire presentation and end on the note you want to end on. Nothing takes the steam out of a presentation more than a Q&A that fizzles out with "that's all the time we have" or "no more questions? Well, thanks for coming."

While Q&A provides an opportunity to demonstrate your mastery of the subject, you don't need to be there all alone.

It can also provide an opportunity to show respect and a collective connection with your audience. Others in the room may know an answer that you don't. "I'm not sure off the top of my head how this would apply to the situation you are describing. How would others among you use what we've been talking about in this gentleman's context?" I continue to be amazed at the great answers others provide. And when they don't, they've bought me enough time to come up with one.

This turn-to-the-audience technique is by far the most powerful way to deal with someone who's just playing "stump the teacher" for the game of it. Let that person's colleagues smack them down on your behalf. In many settings, they know the personalities of the others in your audience. In all cases, the rest of your audience is in a far better position to deal with the disruptive person than you are . . . if you give them permission and the opportunity to do so.

—Warren Evans, trends analyst and business strategist
www.wevans.com

KEY LESSONS FROM CHAPTER 10

1. Q&A time gives you the opportunity to further support your presentation and re-engage your audience. It also enables you to contain questions within a prescribed timeslot.

2. Use TRACT as a tool to stay in control during Q&A time and to turn the session to your advantage.

3. Be selective in your use of TRACT—e.g., it's inappropriate for a one-on-one meeting. The bigger your audience, the more useful it becomes.

4. Be calm during question time and always be polite, even if you're seething with rage.

5. Be careful of allowing people to fire questions at you randomly during your presentation. They may well rearrange your order for you!

6. Never position Q&A at the end. Always have the last say by positioning your conclusion afterward the Q&A section.

7. Be prepared for questions attendees are likely to ask and have some answers prepared in advance.

8. Warn your audience up front that you will set time aside for questions later and that you will end with your conclusion.

9. Factor in enough time for Q&A in case you have to start late and end on time. Question time can be adjusted and can act as a time buffer for you.

10. Concise answers are usually the most convincing answers.

11. Q&A time helps you meet the objectives of your presentation. Do what's necessary to ensure that it serves this purpose.

CHAPTER 11
DEALING WITH LOGISTICS

"It is an experience common to all men to find that, on any special occasion, such as the production of a magical effect for the first time in public, everything that can go wrong will go wrong. Whether we must attribute this to the malignity of matter or to the total depravity of inanimate things, whether the exciting cause is hurry, worry, or what not, the fact remains."

—British stage magician Nevil Maskelyne (1908)

How logistics can ruin a presentation

Perhaps the most significant issue surrounding any form of public speaking is nerves, which was extensively addressed in Chapter Two. By now, you understand clearly some of the main reasons for nervousness. These include inadequate preparation, lack of practice, fear of question time, or intimidation by an audience member.

But another important factor can cause your tension levels to skyrocket if not handled correctly—logistics. Logistics covers anything not related directly to dealing with audience members or to the talk itself. Any experienced presenter will testify to the enormous importance of getting the logistics right and the dire consequences of logistical details going wrong.

Prepare for changing conditions

Having logged up more than 100 recreational dives (that refers to scuba diving, not hanging out in seedy places), I am struck by how different each experience was—even diving in the same spot a few hours later. The lighting could have altered due to incoming cloud cover; the current might have changed direction or intensity; the fish I'd seen two hours before will have swum away. We'd start some dives walking in from shore, others via a backward roll from a "rubber duck" (inflatable boat), and others using a giant stride entry off a large boat. Sometimes we'd do a long, shallow dive; other times, it may be a shorter, deep dive, or a "big blue." Just as each dive is different from the last, so each presentation is different from the previous one. Same goes for venues. It's like when you go diving, you have to set up a whole lot of logistical tactics.

Attention to detail makes the difference between a professional presentation and a shambles. And making sure you get all your ducks in a row means you have to allocate enough time for preparation.

Managing time

Speakers and presenters need to be excellent time managers in the days leading up to the presentation and on the event day itself. Make sure you:

- Set aside enough days to prepare a well-structured presentation.
- Have your presentation flow well rehearsed.
- Make certain your clothes are impeccable (no missing buttons, etc.).
- Check directions and traffic density to the venue the day before.
- Ensure that the venue is suitable in every way for the presentation.
- Check to see you have everything before leaving for the venue.
- Carry spare markers and highlighter pens.
- Allow plenty of time (45 minutes) to check presentation equipment.
- Make sure you are relaxed, comfortable, and composed before starting.
- Know exactly where your backups are, preferably separated from your laptop.

Taking care of audience needs

Just as an evening out at a restaurant can be wrecked by any number of factors not connected to the food, so the success of your presentation rests on factors outside of your presentation itself.

Are the chairs comfortable? Has someone been allocated to get people seated on time so your presentation can begin on time? Have a few chairs been placed near the entrances to seat latecomers with little disruption? Do you know where the restrooms are (not only for you, but in case you are asked)? What time will the breaks begin and end? What will be served at the breaks? Is it part of the package or for purchase? Has the distribution of handouts been arranged? If so, ensure that they are handed out at the end of the presentation and not before. Is there an option for delegates to download or print out your handout afterward? If so, where can they access it?

Setting up at the venue

I once arrived at my seminar venue and was shown by the hotel staff to the Blue Room, which had been set up cinema-style for my talk. I was expecting 50 people and they'd set out about 60 chairs, squashing them together too closely. Since I had 20 minutes to spare, I rearranged the chairs so each audience member could have more space. Once I had the configuration set to my satisfaction, I started setting up my equipment. During my setup, the functions coordinator walked in, introduced herself, and asked if I was Paul du Toit. She then told me my seminar would be held in the Pink Room.

A simple and important lesson: Make sure the person you speak to on arrival knows what's going on. This is particularly important when asking someone whose first language is not the same as yours. It's best to begin by asking to speak to the events coordinator. If he or she is unavailable, ask for someone involved with the main meeting planner. If you aren't convinced that person has been brought up to speed on arrangements, then ask for a duty manager or another more senior person. No harm in asking, more than once, "Are you sure this is the right room?"

Venues can dish up other problematic scenarios and challenges. Be sure to ask questions like these:

1. Is there a stage? Will you be using it? If so, how do you get on to it—from backstage or via stairs? Are the stairs at the side or at the front? (If at the front, be aware that you may temporarily have your back to the audience.)

2. Who will be operating the equipment, you or a technician? If you see a technician on duty when you arrive, don't assume he or she will stay for the entire period. That person may have been hired only to set up. After that, you're on your own. So ask questions and ask the right ones. If the technician leaves shortly after the initial sound check, you may be stuck with a microphone volume that you can't adjust.

3. Has a lectern been provided? If you don't need it, can it be removed, or is it bolted to the floor? Avoid letting it get in your way.

4. What is the lighting configuration? Will there be light on your screen that will affect your slide show? Are there windows behind the screen that may cause a glare through the curtains? Will there be a floodlight shining on you during the presentation? If so, will it "blind" you from

seeing people in the audience? Being able to see them makes a massive difference to your ability to connect with them. On the other hand, the light shining on you should not be so dim that they can't see you clearly.

5. Is the background the same color as the outfit you plan to wear? If so, consider wearing something else so you don't blend into the on-stage background.

6. Is there a time monitor? Is there a system such as green or red lights to give you your time cues? If not, could someone be assigned to give you five-minute and ten-minute warnings before your scheduled time is up so you don't run over? Hint: Many presenters provide their own timers placed at an accessible place.

7. Where will refreshments be available and is the serving configuration appropriate? For example, if you have 120 guests and food tables are set up against the wall for a mid-talk finger buffet, you may have people waiting in lines for some time to get their food. This could easily throw off the schedule. In this case, ask that the tables be moved away from the wall so guests can access food from both sides.

8. If you are the Master of Ceremonies at an event, part of your job is to liaise with the food and beverage manager to ensure that the kitchen is ready when you make food announcements. Who is that person?

It's important to remember that you are the boss: either you, your company, or your client has paid for the use of this venue, and you are entitled to arrange it any way you please. Do not be shy about asking for anything to be changed that doesn't meet with your approval or suit your needs.

Jim Cathcart, past president of NSA-US with more than 30 years of professional speaking experience and more than 2500 presentations behind him, offers this advice regarding setup and logistics:

Once a novice meeting planner came to me at the last minute before my speech and asked, "Do you really need a microphone? Can't you just project a bit more?"

I replied, "No, I don't need a microphone. I will hear every word I say." Then I paused until he realized that the microphone was not for the speaker's benefit. It was for the *audience's* benefit. A look of panic came over him as he admitted he had not arranged for a microphone because he didn't think it would matter very much. He bolted from the room to arrange a microphone. When he returned, he had a desktop radio-station-type microphone with a shoestring tied around it.

I asked, "What's this?" indicating the shoestring. He replied, "You said you wanted a mic you could wear around your neck." (And he was serious!) He actually expected me to "wear" this five-pound microphone!

In the end, I held the heavy item in my hand and delivered my speech. But the microphone choice diminished my ability to do my best. With a good lavaliere or handheld mic, I could have focused on my message and my audience instead of on the equipment.

Speakers are at their best when the audio-visual equipment, the seating arrangements, and the lighting are beneficial to a professional presentation. When they are not, the speaker's attention gets shifted, out of necessity, from the speech to their tools. A noisy room, inadequate cooling or heat, poor lighting, and inappropriate sound equipment are not luxuries for the speaker. They are the tools of the trade.

Since that fiasco with the radio mic, I've used an equipment checklist with every client and reviewed the setup well in advance while corrections could still be made.

Let the speaker do his or her best job. Make the setting and tools fit the task at hand. It's the audience that needs the sound, lighting, and seating, not the speaker.

—Jim Cathcart, founder of Cathcart Institute, Inc.,
author of *The Acorn Principle*
www.cathcart.com

Checking your equipment

I intentionally set aside enough time to check that I have every piece of equipment I will need before I leave home. I also test that it all works in advance, both before I leave home or the office, and at the venue before my talk.

The scope and amount of equipment you need is determined by the size of the venue, the number of people you'll address, and whether you're setting up a slide show. This is part of your initial research and another good reason why you need a reasonable amount of time to set up before participants enter the room.

At certain venues, you may be obliged to use a roof-mounted data projector, but given a choice, I prefer bringing my own. Get a portable one for travel to carry it with you on flights without having to check it. At least you will know that your data projector works and you will have no problem figuring out how to operate it—a great time saver.

On several occasions, I have been promised a data projector at a venue and arrived to find an empty space where it was supposed to be. That's why I always carry my backup projector. There has never been a better time to acquire one. During 2006, the prices of data projectors dropped dramatically. Since 2007, they have been mass-produced and have become very affordable.

I also prefer to use my own remote mouse when I speak using PowerPoint. The model I use fits neatly into the palm of my hand, has a laser pointer, a forward and back button, and can blacken the screen or bring it back again. (See Chapter Seven for the discussion on slide shows.)

Practical Equipment Tip

If your laptop works but the data projector and your speakers don't, check if you've switched on the power on at the wall plug. If your AV (audio visual) support is managed by employees of the venue, that's even more reason to check that the power is on. Your laptop has a battery; your other equipment does not. You don't want your laptop going into hibernation midway through your presentation, so make sure you know how to prevent that from happening.

The one piece of equipment that has proven more problematic than any other is the extension cord. It seems like a low-priority item until you arrive at your venue and realize you've forgotten to bring yours and they haven't provided one. Please believe that their sense of urgency in finding you one is substantially less than yours. I suggest you order one when booking the venue or from the host who books you for the engagement. Then bring one with you just in case, ensuring it has enough adaptors for all your requirements.

I have seen presenters setting up their equipment only to find they have left the cable that joins their receiver to their laptop at their previous presentation. This can create a problem. I always pack up my own paraphernalia after a talk and decline any offers of help. That way I can check that I have not left anything behind. I also know that each item is packed properly, safely, and compactly in its correct place, so I won't have trouble finding anything the next time I need it.

Fix things immediately

If it hasn't happened to you yet, make sure it doesn't. Some piece of equipment breaks or comes loose or batteries go dead at a presentation, then you go home and forget about it. Then, at your next booking, you're about to go live and . . . oops! It could be a button that's come off your favorite suit or dress suit. It could be a loose connection, finding yourself short of an adaptor, or missing batteries in your remote. Be prepared. Keep spare batteries, test your equipment, and check your clothes a few days before the event.

Backing up suggestions

You only really find out the true value of backing up your slide shows when you get stuck without taking care of it. I strongly urge you to follow these suggestions:

1. Back up your most frequently used presentations on a flash drive and on a spare computer. Also do a separate master backup of all your office files on a weekly basis.

2. Ensure that an IT-literate person you trust has separate backups of your shows. Then that person can simply email them to you if something goes wrong when you're away from your base.

3. Have a plan B. You may have to continue without your slides.

4. Remember to refresh your backups when you update your main shows.

5. Ensure that your back-up CDs or flash drives are neatly filed so you have no difficulty finding the show you're looking for quickly.

6. You may also explore secure options available for backing up your shows online.

Expect the best, but prepare for the worst

No matter how well prepared you are, there are dozens of ways your presentation could be undone or affected. Venue problems can be one thing that you can't do anything about; problem people can be another. Here are a few examples of problems you could face:

- Audience members being called out (e.g., doctors, service technicians, emergency personnel)
- Participants eating, drinking alcohol, or arriving intoxicated
- Waiters clearing plates while you're speaking
- A large audience but no amplification system
- Inappropriate seating configuration (e.g., round tables can be awkward in certain situations like a business presentation, or pillars in the room can obscure people's vision)
- Late access to venue, resulting in having to set up in a hurry
- PA system, extension cord, or other piece of equipment arriving late
- People walking in and out during the presentation
- Power outages
- Interruptions like a fire alarm or emergency evacuation
- Venue near or around a noisy construction site
- Outside noise like heavy trucks driving by or aircraft taking off

Some of these circumstances occur before your presentation and others during it. Many are beyond your control yet can have a harrowing effect on your equilibrium, especially if you're delivering a brand new talk.

Naturally, they can cause anxiety. The most critical response is to remain calm and resolve to not let these problems get to you. Be firm in your requirements and don't focus the audience's attention on the problems you're encountering.

In the long run, you may find it efficient and comforting to have an assistant with you who can take care of the logistics and other requirements—that is, those you can delegate!

Travel wisely

Flight delays are becoming more common as traveling by air becomes more congested. I prefer to fly to my destination the day before, especially if I have a morning engagement. Only in the case of late afternoon or evening engagements will I fly the same day, and then it will be a relatively early morning flight. I suggest you give yourself plenty of time in case you face unexpected delays.

Generally, the probability of experiencing delays is greater in the afternoon than early morning. More factors late in the day can contribute, like your aircraft arriving late from its previous destination. Of course, other problems can happen anytime, like inclement weather or technical faults, so building in extra time is always advisable.

When traveling from the airport to your final destination, rely on shuttle transfers only if you have no time pressure or if it's immediately available—and even then, make sure you're not on a multi-stop route with your own destination being last. Usually, it's safer to hire a taxi. The cost is of little consequence compared to the pressure of setting up late or missing a flight.

KEY LESSONS FROM CHAPTER 11

1. Expect conditions to vary considerably from one presentation to the next.

2. Managing your time well makes you a relaxed presenter.

3. The business of a venue is to host as many events as possible, not to ensure that your presentation goes smoothly. That's your job as presenter.

4. Consider audience members and their comfort first. After all, you're doing your talk *for them*, aren't you?

5. Check and test your equipment well in advance. Once your equipment suitcase is packed, don't allow anyone to touch it or borrow items from it.

6. When things break, fall off, or go dead, get the problem fixed as soon as possible. Make a note in your diary or planner to get it handled right after the engagement.

7. Create a system to back up your files regularly and do manual backups of your presentations periodically—as soon as they've been completed. Carry your main backup CD or flash drive separate from your laptop.

8. Always expect the best before your presentation, but be prepared for any eventualities that could upset your equilibrium.

9. Avoid making tight travel arrangements before a presentation. There's not much you can do about bad weather, but you can avoid being caught out by delays of a few hours.

CHAPTER 12
FINISHING TOUCHES

"If you hear that someone is speaking ill of you, instead of trying to defend yourself you should say: 'He obviously does not know me very well, since there are so many other faults he could have mentioned.'"

—Greek Stoic philosopher Epictetus

Introducing the speaker

Every time I speak to an audience, I need a strong introduction and you do, too. Its purpose is to introduce you and the subject of your talk, and to establish credibility and context. This can be accomplished via a pre-recorded audio or video message, but is more often done by the speaker or an assigned introducer.

In most meetings, housekeeping it set up by host, not speaker. But if you're introducing yourself and you also take on the role of the host (for example, you may be conducting a public seminar and you do not have an introducer that day), give a brief introduction of a minute or less that includes starts with the following:

- Welcome
- Logistics (location of refreshment stations, toilets, exits)
- Reminder to mute cell phones
- Times for breaks, etc.

Then pause and introduce yourself, making sure to include the following:

- Presentation title or subject
- Who I am
- Why I'm qualified to speak about this subject

If you're being introduced by someone else, which I recommend, I'd advise you to give that person a script that can be read in 70 to 90 seconds. The script should cover the following key areas:

- Welcome and logistics (if needed)
- Why this subject?
- Why this speaker?
- Why this audience?
- Why now? (That is, why this talk and topic is relevant to this audience at this time.)

Make clear to your introducer the importance of reading your introduction word for word, exactly as you have written it. If you're introducing another speaker, follow the same formula. It's professional and it works. It's practically guaranteed that if you leave it to someone else to formulate an introduction for you, it will either be too long or too short, or it won't include the most appropriate information. Without the correct context being established, you start your talk at a disadvantage.

A good introduction simply helps you put your best foot forward right from the start.

Develop a good outro

What about having a good "outro" planned, too? The outroducer— usually the same person as the introducer—can add tremendous value by *briefly* recapping the main points of the presentation, perhaps adding humor and showing appreciation.

Notice the key word is *briefly*. A long outro can dampen a good talk while a sharp, concise outro can round it off beautifully. Use this opportunity to have the outroducer give a soft promotion of your website, book, services, and other ways your audience can benefit from continued exposure to your message. Some professional speakers regard this as contentious, but my view is that if people have come to listen to your educational talk, you owe it to them to let them know how they can obtain material that assists them in retaining your message. The main issue to me is not whether or not this is done, but how it is done. Generally, an "over the top" sales pitch should be avoided, unless it is done in a humorous manner and complements the context of your presentation.

A good outroducer briefly summarizes a few key points, adds wit, and shows appreciation. The tone should be sincere and enthusiastic, without overdoing the flattery. I'm also uncomfortable with requesting another round of applause for the speaker; it's a bit like begging. The spontaneous applause of the audience was the earned response, so it's best to leave it at that. If the outro is slick and well executed, it may earn a round of applause in its own right.

Don't always expect a walk in the park

Once you've learned the theory, had some practice, and delivered more than one successful presentation while meeting your desired outcomes, you may be forgiven for expecting every engagement to be a walk in the park. The likelihood of this happening is rare. It's like buying a "good" share on the stock exchange after receiving a tip, and then expecting the share price to rise each day without ever going the other way. Well, good shares do indeed dip—in good times and in bad times.

Each presentation brings with it differing conditions and will produce different outcomes. To experience gradual personal improvement as a presenter, you need to keep delivering them, thereby gaining experience. By doing this, you'll find that your failures will teach you more than your successes and you'll continue to improve as you persevere. As with the development of any worthwhile skill, presenting requires ongoing practice and perseverance.

Acknowledge your weaknesses

I've heard that the first step in curing alcoholism is to acknowledge the addiction; only then can one begin the healing process. Without reaching that point of acceptance, no progress is possible. Progress is fuelled by a hunger for improvement, but hindered by delusion.

If you want to learn how to speak to others with impact and persuade them to your way of thinking, accept the truth about where you are now. As you look closely at yourself, pinpoint which factors are helping you succeed and which are standing in your way.

Perhaps you come across a little too intense. Maybe you have a tendency to mumble or waffle. Perhaps you're too complacent. Whatever it may be, you'll only discover your strengths and weaknesses if you take a good look at yourself. When you accurately identify your current position, you have a powerful base for progress. Without a powerful base, your first steps are always tenuous.

The best way to approach your weaknesses is to refer to them as *areas of opportunity*. Because your attitudes guide your brain, the word "weakness" presents a giant mountain to climb. So if you constantly use the word "opportunity" instead, your brain perceives this as being exciting and desirable. It positively affects your brain and can result in much quicker improvement.

Self-Evaluation

Self-evaluation can effectively improve your presentation performance. Your tools are:

- Mirror
- Digital voice recorder
- Camcorder

By using a mirror during practice, you can quickly correct faults relating to body language and clothing. The digital voice recorder allows you to focus on the voice. The camcorder does both, but requires more time and the right logistics to set up and play back. A live audience of one or many will give you other kinds of feedback (e.g., feedback on if the structure makes sense, whether you come across as likeable, and if you are convincing or not).

By frequently evaluating your performance, you will fast-track your improvement as a presenter.

Irritators and other pitfalls

A common trap speakers and presenters fall into is interrupting themselves by saying something unrelated to the point they're attempting to make. This detracts from the impact of the message. Another is apologizing or making excuses, thus diverting attention to the problem rather than the message.

Watch out for irritators. They can be repetitive gestures or fidgeting or words or phrases such as *OK, basically, actually,* or *in terms of.* Irritators can kill your presentation in a few minutes. Practicing should create the awareness of these irritators; experience will help you eliminate them. The trick is to focus consciously on them. Use a digital voice recorder and play it back to see if any irritators creep in too frequently. The occasional "umm" is all right, but it should be infrequent.

Just be yourself

I often encourage people to "just be yourself" when addressing a group of people. Sometimes people mistakenly interpret this advice to mean they should just go ahead and do what's natural—that is, not prepare. *Being yourself* means having the ability to reproduce the way you communicate when you're in a social situation using your voice and your way of speaking. It means not trying to be someone else, unless you use imitation or mimicry in your presentation!

The best way to evaluate the genuineness of your performance is to video yourself in action and play it back to people who know you well. They'll be able to tell you whether they're seeing the authentic "you." It may seem like a tough thing to do, but if being an effective presenter is important enough to you, you should do it.

Remember, the best gift you can give your audience is "you" at your best. After all, they have come to listen to what you have to say, not someone else. Just be yourself.

Phillip van Hooser, a leadership and customer service specialist and NSA-US president for 2009–2010, shares this advice he received early in his career:

About 22 years ago, while I was still contemplating a career in professional speaking, I spoke to a lady who had come into our town to lead a public seminar. As an audience member, I had been mesmerized by her mastery of the platform. She had exhibited complete command of her subject matter; she had been masterful in her use of humor; and her enthusiasm and passion for her topic had been contagious. Not surprisingly, her presentation was a resounding success.

After her presentation, I approached her tentatively and secretly confided that I too had dreams of being a professional speaker. I then asked if she might be willing to offer any helpful advice that would help me make my dream come true. The advice she offered surprised me.

"Don't ever let yourself think of your presentations as presentations," she said. "Instead, approach each presentation as if it is going to be a conversation with friends—even friends you have not met yet—where you have the opportunity to share valuable information that excites you. Then just let your unique personality shine."

As simple as that advice might seem on the surface, I've never forgotten it. In fact, it is the foundation for the mindset I take with me to the platform every time I speak. It has served me well over the past 20 years in more than 2700 professional presentations. Each time I speak, I think, "These are my friends, this information is important, now let's have some fun sharing and learning it together."

The result is this: I don't concern myself with being perfect. I don't worry about comparisons with the speaker before or after me. My mission is simple. I am just there to have a conversation with friends. In the end, people respond.

—Phillip van Hooser, author of *Willie's Way: 6 Secrets for Wooing, Wowing and Winning Customers and Their Loyalty*
www.vanhooser.com

People want you to succeed

Chapter 2 touches on this desire of people wanting you to succeed as a presenter. I would like to expand on that idea here.

For some reason, many of us imagine that when we step up to do our presentations, our audience members wait in keen anticipation for us to make a complete mess of things so they can roar with laughter. Nothing can be further from the truth. Occasionally we do encounter hostile people in our audiences but, for the most part, the majority prefers that those giving presentations give a good account of themselves.

I believe presenting should be a thrilling experience. You potentially have people hanging on your every word, intending to learn from you. What an opportunity! My simple request of you is this: Using pointers in this book to help you, respect their feelings and deliver a message that's truly worthwhile. Don't worry unduly about the content and about yourself. If you've prepared, rehearsed, and you know your flow, you'll be fine. Smile and enjoy the experience. Most important, remember that this presentation is for *them*, not for you. And while I'm on the topic of enjoyment, have fun!

If the opposite of tense is relaxed, then the opposite of fun is misery. When the curtain opens on your presentation, wouldn't it be great for you and everyone in your audience to look as if you're having fun? If people see you enjoy yourself on stage, they'll have fun, too. It relaxes them, increases your connectivity to them, and gives you the best chance of meeting your presentation objectives. Make the decision to have fun up front. In fact, make that decision *now*. Whenever you present, build in fun. You owe it to yourself— and to your audiences.

The final touch

Having facilitated presentation skills many times and delivered hundreds of paid speeches, I have a distinct sense of where I was when I started and what it took to get to where I am now. I firmly believe that all who can speak a language have the ability to either make a speech or deliver a presentation in that language— provided they take the job of preparation seriously but not take themselves too seriously! I further believe we owe it to our audiences to create a presentation that's worth setting aside time to hear and understand.

When you go shopping, you don't want to come home empty handed, right? That's frustrating. Every member of your audience feels the same. These people have given you the opportunity to convince them—to "buy" your ideas. It's your duty to oblige them and make their shopping trip successful.

> "Aspire to acquire the desire you admire. But if in the process you perspire, don't retire but refire to acquire the desire you admire."
>
> —Author unknown

KEY LESSONS FROM CHAPTER 12

1. Write and print out your introduction before your talk and ask your introducer to read it word for word—or, if he or she has time, memorize it.

2. It may be appropriate to prepare a written "outro," too—particularly if you want your closing message reinforced by someone else.

3. Because each presentation is given under different conditions to different audiences, expect that you may not get better every time. Sometimes, what you've done in the past won't work for you in a new situation. This doesn't mean you're slipping, only that you're learning. Your failures teach you more than your successes.

4. Understanding your current strengths and opportunity areas (weaknesses) will fast track your improvement.

5. Whether you use a mirror, a digital voice recorder, a camcorder, or a live audience (or a combination of these) to evaluate yourself, get feedback at

your rehearsals. Doing live performances is invaluable for improving your presentation quickly.

6. Irritators and regular self-interruption can destroy even a well-structured presentation. Getting feedback (see #5) when you practice will help you eliminate these presentation gremlins.

7. The best performance you can possibly deliver will reflect *you*. By all means, learn from the best, but don't copy others. Instead, emulate *you*.

8. It's rare to encounter audience members who would like to see you fail. Almost always, they want you to succeed. Believing this alone should help build your confidence. I rely on this principle, without anyone's permission, every single time I present.

9. Imagine you're simply having a conversation with friends when giving your talk. Under these favorable conditions, become as enthusiastic about what you're saying as the occasion warrants.

10. Having fun while you present rubs off on audience members and puts them in the mood to make the right decision.

11. Having come to listen to you, people *deserve* hearing a great presentation. Make sure you give it to them.

ACKNOWLEDGMENTS

This work would not have been possible without the support of my wife and business associate Trudi—no mean presentation skills facilitator herself—who endured my many late nights of writing and editing the manuscript. The Congruence Team, my loyal Office Manager Ninette Rex, and Operations Manager Henry Coetzer have been my constants.

Without the continual encouragement of Dan Poynter, himself the author of over 120 books and the godfather of thousands more, this book might still be a pipe dream.

My sister, Michelle Coetzee, who tirelessly edited the initial manuscript several times and added vital components to Chapter 8, came with a bonus or two. As an accomplished actress, playwright, storyteller, training facilitator, and press editor, she brought special insights into many aspects of this subject. In her careful editing, she took pains to retain my particular style of communication, giving this work added authenticity. Her patience and her perseverance was commendable.

At the beginning, when I wavered, Barbara McNichol encouraged and cajoled me to keep my momentum going. Without her, this book may still be merely a collection of articles and tips.

Barbara worked with me on the final edit and undoubtedly helped me create a better book.

When I first asked Mark Sanborn, CSP*, CPAE**, to write the foreword for me, the proviso was that once he'd carefully read the script, he would decide whether he would do it or not. I'm grateful to him that he decided in favor of writing it!

Each chapter of this book contains additional insights from carefully selected subject experts from around the world, all accomplished speakers in their own right and many of them authors too. They are Simon T. Bailey, CSP; Paul Bridle, CSP; Alvin Law CSP, HoF***; Lesley Everett; Haydee Antezana; Marilyn Snyder; Marija Ruygrok; Clive Simpkins; Alan Stevens, FPSA****; Maria Farrugia; Warren Evans, CSP; Jim Cathcart, CSP, CPAE; Phillip van Hooser, CSP, HoF; and Professor Ronald Arden. When asked to contribute to this book, not one of them missed a beat in agreeing.

I have no doubt that every one of them yearns, as I do, for the day when being able to stand up and speak with confidence to an audience is no longer the domain of the few.

Those in one last group are really the unsung heroes of this work—the many hundreds of delegates who have attended our presentation skills programs. Without the privilege of working with every one of them, this book would have been a poorer effort, devoid of the understanding that comes with participative interaction.

My sincere gratitude and thanks to you all!

—Paul du Toit

* CSP—Certified Speaking Professional
** CPAE—Member, Speaker Hall of Fame
*** HoF—Canadian Speaker Hall of Fame
**** FPSA—Fellow Professional Speakers Association UK

ABOUT THE AUTHOR

PAUL DU TOIT is a Certified Speaking Professional* and an experienced presentation skills facilitator. Since 1999, he has trained and addressed thousands of people on presentation skills and frequently lectures at universities on this topic. He speaks on motivation, customer service, mind-set shift, and platform skills nationally and internationally.

A founding member and past president of the Professional Speakers Association of Southern Africa (2005–2006), Paul has also served as the secretary of the International Federation for Professional Speakers (2006–2008), now Global Speakers Federation.

Currently, Paul is managing director of the South Africa-based Congruence Group, which develops human capital within companies of all sizes.

*As of January 2011, the Certified Speaking Professional (CSP) designation is held by fewer than 700 professional speakers globally, which is fewer than 10 percent of professional speakers worldwide. Only two national speakers associations within the Global Speakers Federation (GSF) are licensed to award the CSP designation—the United States and Australia.

Information about Paul and his organization can be found at:

http://www.pauldutoit.net

http://www.presentationskills.co.za

http://www.congruence.co.za

mailto:director@congruence.co.za

The Certified Speaking Professional designation is the most sought-after and visible measure of professionalism in the speaking business internationally. It demonstrates professional standards in four key areas:

- Association membership
- Continuing education
- Speaking performance
- Business management

Paul du Toit is only the second South African to be awarded a CSP designation and the first since 1984. Many contributors to this book also hold this designation. For more information, go to any of the following websites:

http://www.nsaspeaker.org (under Certification)

http://www.nsasouthafrica.co.za (under Membership)

http://www.nationalspeakers.asn.au (under Designations)

http://www.iffps.org